# Outer Banks Cuisine
# A Sampling of Our Restaurants
## With
## Recipes

by Becky Smith

# Outer Banks Cuisine
## A Sampling of Our Restaurants With Recipes


Third Printing 2000


Published by: Becky Smith, Dirt Enterprises
P.O. Box 262
Harbinger, N.C. 27941
(252) 491-2403

Cover: by Vicki Wallace
Manteo, N.C.

ISBN: 0-9662656-3-7

Printed in the USA by

3212 East Highway 30 • Kearney, NE 68847 • 1-800-650-7888

# Introduction

Covering 391 square miles of land and 800 square miles of water, North Carolina's Outer Banks (Barrier Islands) stretch from the northern most beaches of Corolla to Ocracoke Island. The Outer Banks long lay in a state of isolation but have undergone a radical transformation in natural character since first sighted by early European explorers. In the days of early settlers the Banks were covered with dense forests as settlers cut the trees to build their homes and boats, the sand was no longer held in place by vegetation. The winds and storms began to move the sand, killing the trees, thus the process continued until the 1930s. The Civilian Conservation Corps then erected sand fences and planted trees and grass on the Outer Banks for stabilization of the dunes.

There were no bridges from the mainland until 1931 and paved roads did not extend the full length of the islands until the early 1950s. Even today, areas north of Corolla can only be reached by traveling on the beach.

The original descendents of many Outer Banks families were shipwrecked mariners that were washed up on the shores of these islands. Many of these men were of English decent. Today, an Elizabethan accent continues to survive on the Outer Banks. High tide is pronounced "hoi toide" and fried seafood is "froid" seafood. History abounds on these stretches of barrier islands.

With so many interesting things to do and places to visit and the wide array of eating establishments to choose from, vacationers will have a hard time deciding what to do first. A handful of tiny fishing villages, miles of pristine beaches, and some of the country's most significant historic sites are located here. The Cape Hatteras National Seashore stretches for 75 miles along the Atlantic Ocean and is the largest undeveloped coastline along the East Coast. Here you will find the famous Cape Hatteras Lighthouse (built in 1870) that stands 208 feet tall, the black and white striped lighthouse is the tallest brick lighthouse in the United States. In 1999, the historic lighthouse had to be moved inward 2,900 feet due to the encroaching ocean less than 120 feet from its base. The journey took 23 days. On November 13, 1999 the Cape Hatteras Lighhouse once again resumed her duty of flashing nightime warning of dangerous waters. The relocation of the lighthouse has been called "the move of the century" and is an engineering feat that has fascinated millions.

Roanoke Island—Fort Raleigh National Historic Site— the site of the first English settlement in North America should be on your list of places to visit. The Lost Colony outdoor drama tells "History's greatest mystery" of the brave colony of English pioneers of 1587 who encountered natives of a strange new -world but later vanished without a trace.

Seafood is probably one of the biggest draws for the Outer Banks. Offshore fishing and sound fishing by the local watermen offers a variety of fish such as dolphin, wahoo, tuna, king mackerel, shrimp, oysters, and many others. Many of the local restaurants buy their fresh seafood locally.

The Outer Banks has a wide array of restaurants from which to choose, offering every type of food to please every palate and prices to suit everyone's wallet. Restaurateurs open around early March, April and are increasingly staying open longer into the fall each year. The off-seasons have become very popular for dining out because of the same great food and friendly service with a lot less crowds to deal with. There are upscale cafes with European ambiance and restaurants with extraordinary culinary creations and some with just plain good food.

I hope you will enjoy this book and some of the culinary secrets of the award winning restaurants as a guide to some of the best restaurants on the Outer Banks with special recipes from their chefs.

*Cape Hatteras Lighthouse*

*Buxton, NC*

# 1587 Restaurant

Queen Elizabeth Avenue
Manteo, North Carolina

Donnie Just, General Manager (252) 473-1587
Donny King & Susan Holton-Rodgers-Executive Chefs
TJ Shillingsford, Sous Chef
Tranquil House In (252) 473-1404

1587 Restaurant is located in the Tranquil House Inn on the Manteo waterfront. Just minutes from the special attractions, old and new, found in Manteo, they provide an atmosphere that is both comfortable and intriguing. Upon entering the restaurant, you will find exciting food and interesting wines paired with a professional and upbeat level of service. Their chefs offer creative twists to familiar foods including fresh local ingredients. Southern Living describes it a "remarkably creative cuisine." Their wine list has also been recognized in Wine Spectator with their annual "Award of Excellence." In an area where locals know and value great restaurants, their friendly staff is proud to offer a product well respected. This recipe is one of many unique dishes you can learn about when you sit near their open kitchen and view the skilled and dramatic creation of their cuisine.

They are as equally proud of their restaurant, and the service it provides, as they are the Tranquil House Inn. You will find a beautiful twenty-five room bed and breakfast with individually decorated rooms and many fine amenities. After dinner, stroll along the marina and admire the charming and comfortable surroundings, or finish the night with an evening libation on their large open deck overlooking Shallowbag Bay.

Reservations are highly recommended in season.

## *Outer Banks Greentail Shrimp in a Mediterranean Chardonnay Broth*

2 oz. olive oil
1 T. salt & pepper
20 ct. Greentail shrimp, peeled and deveined
½ ct. yellow onions, medium dice
½ ct. red peppers, medim dice
½ ct. green peppers, medium dice
6 ct. Crimini mushrooms, sliced
4 ct. artichoke hearts, quartered
1 oz. fresh garlic, minced
2 sprigs fresh sage, chopped
6 leaves fresh basil, chiffonade
1 c. Chardonnay
2 c. fish stock
2 ct. Roma tomatoes, halved and sliced
4 oz. feta cheese, crumbled

*In place of shrimp stock, if not already made, use canned clam juice.

In a 2-quart capacity sauce pan, cook the shrimp, onions, peppers and mushrooms in the olive oil and salt and pepper until halfway cooked, stirring occasionally. Add the mushrooms, artichoke hearts, garlic and herbs, and stir on medium heat for 2 minutes. Next, add the Chardonnay and boil on high heat until reduced by half. Then add the shrimp stock and Roma tomatoes and simmer for a minute or two. Finally, add the crumbled feta cheese and ladle into four soup bowls to be served immediately. Yields 4 portions.

# 3RD Street Oceanfront Grille

Sea Ranch Quality inn
1731 N. Virginia Dare Trail (Beach Road), MP 7
Kill Devil Hills, North Carolina
Jason Rodriguez, Executive Chef (252) 441-7126

*3rd Street Grille offers an unparalleled ocean view. A wall of glass reveals a view that makes you feel as if you are in the sea spray. This year will bring many changes including a bi-yearly menu. 3rd Street will offer more of an International cuisine while not losing sight of their Southern roots.*

*The menu features traditional Outer Banks seafood prepared with a Southern regional flair. Steaks, pan-seared shrimp and sweet peppers with red eye gravy over cheese grits are just a few of the items on the menu. A children's menu and nightly specials are available. Breakfast and dinner are served daily in season.*

## Shrimp and Pork Spring Rolls

### with Rice Stick Noodle, Romaine Lettuce and Ponzo Sauce

*Ingredients 1:*

2 lbs. ground pork
2 lbs. ground shrimp
1½ medium onions, small dice
2 T. minced ginger
2 T. minced garlic

*Ingredients 2:*

1 c. shredded green cabbage
1 c. shredded carrot
¼ c. chopped cilantro
2 green onions, sliced

*Ponzo Dipping Sauce:*

¼ c. soy sauce
¼ c. rice wine vinegar
¼ c. sesame oil
¼ c. Vietnamese fish sauce

Spring Roll wrappers (can substitute won-ton or eggroll wrappers, but will need to be fried).

Sauté onion in vegetable oil until soft, add ginger and garlic; and cook 2 minutes longer. Add ground shrimp and pork. Cook thoroughly. Add Ponzo Sauce, heat through. Pour pork and shrimp mixture over vegetables. Let sit for 30 minutes. Roll pork mixture in Spring Roll wrappers, bake in oven until golden brown. Serve with rick stick noodle and chiffonade of Romaine lettuce.

# Awful Arthur's

2106 N. Virginia Dare Trail MP 6
Kill Devil Hills, North Carolina
Jay Whitehead, Owner (252) 441-5955
Kenny McLean, Chef

A favorite local and tourist spot across from the Avalon Pier, Arthur's is always busy no matter the time of year. Know as the "Home of the Happy Oyster" this raw bar promises a good time and great food. Awful Arthur's is a very casual place where seafood is the specialty. A large menu featuring everything from soups and salads, scallops, lobster, oysters, clams, burgers, a backfin burger with backfin crabmeat, and sandwiches are available. Look for the daily entrée specials posted on the large boards.

Enjoy the beautiful ocean views while you sip your favorite beverage in the upstairs lounge. Several varieties of beer or on tap and a full line of liquor and specialty drinks are available. Night's are always extremely busy. Mondays are Local's Nights featuring food and drink specials. Don't forget to pick up one of Awful Arthur's famous T-shirts. Open year-round for lunch and dinner.

## She Crab-Lobster Bisque

4 oz. butter, unsalted
1 large onion, roughly chopped
1 medium carrot, peeled, roughly chopped
1 clove garlic, minced
1 ½ T. paprika
½ T. Awful Arthur's Crab Spice or Old Bay
2/3 cup all-purpose flour
1 qt. clam juice
1 tsp. Tabasco sauce
1 T. Worcestershire
1 pt. heavy cream
black pepper, freshly cracked, to taste
6 oz. backfin crabmeat, picked through
4 oz. Lobster meat, cleaned, and diced
1 oz. dry sherry

Method

1. Melt the butter and sauté the onions, carrots, and garlic until tender.
2. Add the paprika and Awful Arthur's Crab Spice and cook for 1 minute.
3. Add the flour to make a roux and cook 1-2 minutes, stirring constantly
4. Add the clam juice, Tabasco, Worcestershire, and heavy cream, whisking well to incorporate the roux. Bring to a boil and turn off the heat
5. Puree in batches in a blender and season to taste with the black pepper
6. Add the crabmeat, lobster and sherry, and mix well
7. Serve with freshly chopped parsley

Yield: 8 each 8 oz. bowls

## *Lobster Stuffed Avocados*

3 Lobster tails
1/4 lb. butter
2 T. onions finely chopped
2 tsp. Paprika
2/3 cup Sherry
2/3 cup Cognac
1/4 cup flour
1 cup heavy cream
1/4 cup lemon juice
Cayenne pepper, Garlic, Nutmeg
salt and white pepper to taste
12 Avocados
3/4 cup Parmesan cheese
Bread crumbs, minced parsley and lemon wedges for garnish

Remove meat from tails and cut into bite-size pieces. Sauté onion in butter. Add lobster and heat until almost all liquid is evaporated 1-2 minutes. Sprinkle with paprika, add sherry and cognac, simmer 5 minutes. Sprinkle with flour and mix well. Add heavy cream and simmer, stirring until thickened. Add lemon juice and other seasonings to your taste. Set aside. Halve avocados, remove pits and arrange in a buttered casserole dish. Stuff each half with lobster mixture. Fold whipped cream into 2 cups of hollandaise sauce and pour over the avocados, sprinkle with fresh parmesan and bread crumbs. Bake at 350 degrees for 10-15 minutes or until tops are brown. Serve on warm platter with parsley sprigs and lemon wedges. Makes a nice, colorful appetizer.

# *The Back Porch Restaurant*

*1324 Country Rd.*
*Ocracoke Island, North Carolina*
*Daphne Bennink, Owner* (252) 928-6401

*The Back Porch Restaurant offers some of the island's finest cuisine. Screen porch dining in an elegant atmosphere or eating in one of the small nooks or large open dining room will surely complete a memorable evening on this picturesque island.*

*The menu features fresh vegetables, herbs, and local caught seafood. All breads, sauces, and desserts are made fresh in the Back Porch kitchen daily. The crab cakes with sweet red pepper sauce is outstanding as is the bourbon pecan chicken breast rolled in pecans, with a bourbon butter sauce. In addition to the outstanding entrees, you won't want to miss trying the crab beignets or one of the restaurants most popular appetizers, Back Porch asiago terrine served with toast rounds. Leave room for some of their fabulous homemade desserts. A great wine and imported beer selection is available.*

*Its well worth the trip including the ferry ride, just to eat at this great restaurant. Dinner is served nightly in season.*

## *Back Porch Asiago Terrine*

1 lb. Asiago cheese, grated
1 lb. cream cheese
1/3 cup best quality mayonnaise
2 T. roasted garlic, minced or pureed
3/4 cup chopped fresh basil
1 1/3 cup sun dried tomatoes, soaked and chopped coarse
1 teaspoon pepper

Cream cheeses and mayonnaise together, add the rest of the ingredients until blended. Serve warm with toasted walnuts. Terrine can also be served at room temperature as a spread.

# Basnight's Lone Cedar Cafe

Nags Head/Manteo Causeway
Nags Head, North Carolina

Sandy & Marc Basnight, Owners (252) 441-5405
Bud Gruninger, Executive Chef

*Ever since the Lone Cedar Cafe opened its doors in 1996, it has been a favorite for tourists and locals alike. Incredible views of the Roanoke Sound can be seen from every table in this casual, upscale eatery. The cafe is decorated with fishing memorabilia, duck decoys, and hunting items reminiscent of the old Lone Cedar Hunt Club of bygone era for which this eatery is named.*

*This cafe specializes in regional eastern North Carolina foods using only local fresh vegetables and seafood. Appetizers, salads, soups, sandwiches, seafood and other specials of the day are served for lunch. For dinner, try one of the seafood dishes or the certified Angus beef, or pastas, or one of the great nightly specials. A full bar with an extensive wine list is available. Save room for some great homemade desserts. Lunch and dinner is served daily from February through November.*

## Sausage & Shrimp Pasta

2 oz. extra virgin olive oil
3 T. chopped fresh garlic
½ lb. cooked Hot Italian sausage, sliced
1½ lbs. jumbo shrimp,
peeled & deveined (green tails)
4 oz. mushrooms (shiitake, portabella, button)
2 Roma tomatoes, diced
2 bunch scallions, diced
2 oz. white wine (dry)
2 oz. chicken stock
2 T. butter
Grated black pepper
1½ lbs. angel hair pasta
Romano cheese

In large sauté pan, heat olive oil. Add garlic, sausage, shrimp and mushrooms, and saute 2 minutes. Add tomatoes and scallions, and saute 1 minute. Add wine, chicken stock, pepper and butter, and simmer 2 minutes. Serve over pasta and top with Romano cheese. Serves 4.

# *Billy's Fish House Restaurant*

*Highway 12 (on the harbor)*
*Buxton, North Carolina*
*Billy & Chalaron May, Owners* *(252) 995-5151*

*If you are looking for a black tie restaurant, Billy's is probably not for you; but if you are looking for a restaurant that provides seafood dishes cooked in the traditional Outer Banks style, you won't be disappointed. Thirty years ago this restaurant was a "fish house." Look closely and you will notice that the floor slants toward the sound. This was done on purpose so the water from the fish boxes would drain back into the sound.*

*Billy is a down-home type person ("good ole boy") with an easy going manner. He does like to eye the pretty girls. It is rumored that Chalaron breaks a rolling pin a week just to keep him in check.*

*Visit Billy's. You will have a fun time, eat good food, and add a pleasant memory to your Outer Banks adventure.*

## *Shrimp Pasta Salad*

2 lbs. fresh shrimp, cooked & chopped
½ c. celery, chopped
2 hard boiled eggs, chopped
1½ T. Old Bay seasoning
½ c. chopped green peppers
1 T. dill weed
8 oz. shell pasta, cooked according to package instructions
1 large bottle "Hidden Valley" Ranch dressing
½ c. mayonnaise

Mix all ingredients together, toss, and refrigerate for 4 hours. Makes at least 6 generous servings.

# Black Pelican Seafood Company

3848 Virginia Dare Trail, MP 4
Kitty Hawk, North Carolina
(252) 261-3171

This is one of the favorite restaurants for locals on the Outer Banks with oceanfront dining and open all year serving lunch and dinner. A new addition was added in 1998 with more oceanfront seating and a deck for dining while enjoying the waves. With the addition of the new gift shop, patrons can purchase prints, books, jewelry, t-shirts and many other fine items. The ambiance is upbeat and casual. The raw bar is a great place to gather and try some of the great appetizers and drinks. Try one of the wood-fired gourmet pizzas; one of my favorites is the White Seafood or the Aloha.

Lunch includes a list of daily specials that are awesome. Sandwiches and salads are also served. The dinner menu offers entrees such as Grilled Salmon topped with lemon dill butter, Baked shrimp and crab with beurre blanc sauce, prime rib, Kansas City Strip. All entrees are served with seasonal vegetables, red potatoes, and homemade turkish pita bread. Dinner specials are served nightly. Save room for the desserts; these are to die for. Children's menu is also available.

## Seviche

1 lb. conch
2 chopped onions
2 c. lime juice
½ c. cook oil
¼ c. capers, drained
4 tsp. sugar
3 tsp. crushed red peppers
½ tsp. salt
1 T. cilantro or parsley

Place conch meat and onion in plastic bag--place bag in bowl. For marinade, combine juice, oil, capers, sugar, red pepper, and salt. Pour over fish and onions. Close bag and marinate in refrigerator at least 24 hrs., turning occasionally. Add cilantro about 1½ hrs. before serving.

# Blue Parrot Café

Route 2, Castaways Hotel
Avon, North Carolina

Betty and Bill Horan, Owners (252) 995-6993
Page and Casey Lewis, Owners Casey Lewis, Chef

*The Blue Parrot Café will be entering its 7th year on the Outer Banks. Their reputation for great food, service and personnel that take pride in this restaurant all add up to a fine dining experience for even the most discriminating diner. The wonderful food is served in a gaily decorated dining room, with an eclectic blend of antiques, rattan, hanging parrots, plants, and original paintings and photographs.*

*Chef Casey Lewis, trained by Johnson and Wales, offers an enticing menu specializing in blackened seafood (tuna wahoo, shrimp or scallops), steamed seafood (lobster, shrimp, scallops), and excellent beef (Best prime rib on the island, delmonicos and filet mignon). Favorite entrees among diners are filet mignon stuffed with lump crabmeat and smothered in béarnaise sauce and the ever-popular blackened tuna with salsa shrimp. The homemade key lime pie and chocolate pecan pie have fans all up and down the East Coast. Chef Lewis makes excellent she-crab soup that keeps the patrons returning time after time. The Café also offers $9.99 meals for the thrifty diner.*

*A small sports bar area, complete with satellite dish, is loaded with sports memorabilia. Things start hopping early with 10 cent shrimp every day from 4 to 7. A kiddie menu is available. Open daily in-season for breakfast, dinner.*

## Chocolate Pecan Pie

2 ounces unsweetened chocolate
3 T. butter
1 cup light corn syrup
¾ cup sugar
½ tsp. salt
3 eggs, slightly beaten
1 tsp. vanilla
1 cup chopped pecans
1 9-inch unbaked pie shell

Preheat oven to 350 degrees. In double boiler, melt chocolate and butter, in a separate pan simmer syrup and sugar for 2 minutes. Add chocolate mixture and cool lightly. Add salt to eggs. Slowly dribble chocolate mixture into eggs, stirring constantly. Blend in vanilla and nuts. Pour into shell and bake at 375 degrees for 35 minutes. Top with homemade whipped cream and chocolate syrup. Pie is great served warm!

# The Blue Point Bar & Grill

The Waterfront Shops
N.C. Hwy 12
Duck, North Carolina

Sam McGann & John Power, Owners (252) 261-8090
Thomas Power & Kris Mullins, Owners
Thomas Power, Executive Chef

In 1989 John Power and Sam McGann opened The Blue Point Bar & Grill in the small quaint village of Duck, North Carolina. It was an immediate success with local homeowners and tourists alike looking for a contemporary taste of the Outer Banks. Situated among a cluster of shops along a boardwalk, this "gourmet diner" offers an expansive view of the Currituck Sound. The 1950s-style interior is energized with glass blocks, black and white tile floors, chrome finishes, and red upholstery. An enclosed porch overlooks the sound and provides an incredible view of the sunset.

The Blue Point has been recognized for their excellence in cuisine by such publications as Gourmet, Bon Apetit, Southern Living, Food Arts and many others. In 1995 and 1996, Wine Spectator magazine awarded an "Award of Excellence" for their in-house wine list. The Blue Point as well as Ocean Boulevard received a 3-star rating from the Mobil Guide.

The Blue Point is open seven days a week year-round, serving eclectic cuisine for lunch, dinner and brunch on Sundays. Dinner reservations are highly recommended and can be accepted up to one week in advance. This restaurant is a must-do on the Outer Banks.

## *Scallops Poached in Olive Oil with Rosemary, Black Olives, Roasted Garlic & Lemon*

12 large sea scallops
8 cloves roasted garlic
1 bunch fresh rosemary
12 large Kalamata black olives
4 wedges lemon
½ c. olive oil
Salt & pepper to taste

Clean the scallops of the small muscle and pat dry. In a cast iron skillet over medium heat, bring olive oil to 300 degrees. Add scallops, roasted garlic and rosemary.

The technique is to poach, not fry, the scallops, so watch the temperature so as not to cook the scallops too quickly; but allow to simmer for 1-2 minutes. Then add black olives. Turn scallops, continue to cook 1-2 minutes longer until scallops are just cooked through. Remove skillet from heat. Add a squeeze of fresh lemon juice. Serves 4.

*To Plate: Place on each dish three scallops, roasted garlic, black olives and a spoonful of the seasoned olive oil. Serve with lemon wedges. Toasted french bread croutons or rosemary foccacia would accompany this plate nicely.*

# Bluewater Grill & Wine Bar

Highway 12
Waves, North Carolina

Rick Powell & Holly Blakemore, Owners (252) 987-1300
Lou Petrozza, Chef

*The Bluewater Grill and Wine Bar specializes in aged Angus beef and fresh seafood cooked over a real mesquite wood fire. Steaks are cut to order and only top quality ingredients are used in the kitchen. When a recipe calls for Parmesan cheese, only imported Italian Reggiano is used. Filet Mignon may be ordered stuffed with French Roquefort. Also on the menu are a variety of pasta dishes, local shellfish, live lobster, homemade soups, salads, and desserts. The dining rooms are situated to enjoy stunning views of the Pamlico Sound (especially at Sunset!) as well as the large herb garden in the back which provides fresh and unusual enhancements to the daily fare. The grilled Wahoo steaks below use skewers from two huge rosemary bushes which mark the entrance to the garden. This dish also features one of Chef Petrozza's special sauces.*

## Grilled Rosemary Skewered Wahoo with Raspberry Beurre Blanc

Strip the foliage from several medium-sized fresh rosemary twigs. Push the stems through the flesh of the Wahoo steaks and grill. The Wahoo will be infused with a wonderfully fragrant flavor. Serve with the Raspberry sauce, prepared as follows:

In a small sauce pan place:

- 1 T. minced shallots
- ½ c. white wine
- ½ c. white wine vinegar
- ½ c. fresh raspberries

Reduce over high heat until almost dry. Add ½ cup heavy cream and reduce to half volume. Add ½ stick of butter cut into small pieces, stirring constantly with a whisk until thickened. Serve over Rosemary Grilled Wahoo steaks.

# *Cafe Atlantic*

*P.O. Box 123, N.C. Hwy. 12*
*Ocracoke, North Carolina*
*Bob & Ruth Toth, Owners* (252) 928-4861

*This upscale and casual restaurant is located in a traditional beach-style building, but don't let that fool you. There is nothing traditional about the innovative way this restaurant prepares and serves their delicious, mouth-watering fares.*

*The views out across the marsh grasses and dunes is fantastic. The gallery-like effect is produced by the hand-colored photographs of local artist and writer, Ann Ehringhaus.*

*The lunch menu includes salads and sandwiches, while the dinner menu offers combinations of fresh seafood, a wide range of beef, chicken, and pasta plates. Sunday brunches are from 11 a.m. to 3 p.m. Champagne and mimosas are always served. Make sure to save room for their outstanding desserts; this is to top off a delicious meal.*

## *Sweet Potato Biscuits*

2 medium-sized sweet potatoes (about 1¼ lbs.)
½ c. unsalted butter, melted (1 stick)
¼ c. golden brown sugar (packed)
2¼ c. all-purpose flour
1 T. baking powder
¼ tsp. salt
½ tsp. baking soda
¼ tsp. ground cinnamon
⅔ c. buttermilk

Preheat oven to 400 degrees. Pierce potatoes in several places using a fork. Bake potatoes for about 1 hour until very tender. Cut potatoes in half and scoop out the pulp from the skins. Put potato pulp in a small bowl and cool completely. Reduce the oven temperature to 375 degrees. Place 1 cup sweet potato in a bowl, add brown sugar and butter, and beat until smooth. Sift flour, baking powder, salt, baking soda, and cinnamon into medium bowl. Mix dry ingredients into sweet potato mixture alternately with buttermilk, in 3 additions, beginning and ending with dry ingredients. Transfer dough to generously floured surface. Roll to ¼-inch thickness. Using a 2¼-inch round cookie cutter, cut out biscuits. Arrange on baking sheet. Gather scraps into ball, re-roll to ¼ inch thick and cut out additional biscuits. Arrange on baking sheet. Bake biscuits until golden about 25 minutes. Makes about 12.

# Carolina Seafood

2042 N. Virginia Dare Trail (Beach Road), MP 6½
Kill Devil Hills, North Carolina
Carol Ann Angelos, Owner (252) 441-6851
JoAnn Davis, Manager
Danny Greeson, Chef

*Carolina Seafood is a fun, relaxed buffet restaurant with an ocean view and a beachy surfside feel. It is great for families, kids, couples, vacationers and anyone who enjoys fresh local seafood and some "land lover" items in a casual atmosphere.*

*Crack crablegs or Blue crabs, peel shrimp and enjoy your favorite beverage while catching up with that relative or friend you have not had time to chat with back home.*

*It is important to them to serve good food and have customers leave happy and full. So come and join them. If you have to wait for a table, which is typical in season, sit back on their porch or grab a picnic table and take in the view and a breeze.*

*They look forward to serving you.*

## Seafood Bisque

| | |
|---|---|
| 2 qts. water | 1 onion |
| 1 qt. half and half | 1 lb. shrimp or crabmeat |
| 4 c. flour | 1 T. parsley |
| 1 lb. butter | 1 T. gran garlic |
| 2 large carrots | 1 T. fine ground pepper |
| 4 stalks celery | 4 oz. base (seafood-crab-clam) |

Make Roux from butter and flour and thicken.

Bring 2 qts. of water to boil and add finely chopped celery, carrots, onion and seasonings. Bring to boil again and add seafood. Bring back to boil and add base and half and half. Before it boils again, mix in Roux and whip in while it comes to a boil. It is ready. Three-fourths cup of cooking sherry may be added now if desired.

# Chilli Peppers Restaurant

3001 N. Croatan Hwy., MP 5½
Kill Devil Hills, North Carolina
Jim Douglas, Owner (252) 441-8081

*This is the spot you've been looking for, serving creative cooking with a Southwestern flair with taste from around the world. The menu changes frequently, with daily lunch and dinner specials offered. Chilli Peppers is a casual, fun place with entertainment here going on late at night. A full bar is separated from the dining area and offers a nice wine selection, margaritas, and a variety of beer.*

*Some of my favorite entrees are the Peanut-Cilantro Crusted Tuna Steak, and the Creamy Green Chili Jumbo Lump Crabmeat Enchilada Stack with spiced rice, black beans and sour cream cocktail sauce. Try the nachos appetizer; it's a meal in itself.*

*Chilli Peppers is a four-time winner of the Outer Banks Association Chowder Cookoff. They received the prestigious Scovie Award for their award-winning Cantaloupe Habanero Hot Sauce and have won many other International awards.*

*Lunch and dinner are served seven days a week year round. Weekend brunches feature a Sunday Bloody Mary Brunch. Be sure and take home a bottle of Chilli's award-winning hot sauces.*

## Chimmi Churry Oysters

*For Chimmi Churry:*

¼ lb. fresh cilantro
4 bunch green onions
1 T. minced garlic
6 c. olive oil
2 T. chicken base
2 T. salt
1 T. black pepper

Mix all ingredients together in blender or food processor. Sauté 1 dozen shucked oysters in 2 T. butter. Add desired amount of Chimmi Churry and bring to boil. Plate and sprinkle with shredded fresh Parmesan and garnish with toast points. Yields 8 cups.

# *Clara's Seafood Grill*

*The Waterfront Shops*
*Manteo, North Carolina*
*Peaches Shannon Woodard, Owner* (252) 473-1727

*Dine on the historic waterfront overlooking Shallowbag Bay and the state ship, Elizabeth II. View the many boats and yachts that line the waterfront daily. Watch Kayaks glide through the waters while you dine and people stroll the boardwalk.*

*Clara's has a casual, relaxing atmosphere and serves up the freshest seasonal foods grilled to perfection. Meals are accompanied by the best sweet cornbread ever eaten. All the dinners are excellent with grilled fish specials offered daily. The lunch menu offers delicious sandwiches, salads and specials posted on the board daily. The she-crab soup is the best you'll find anywhere on the Outer Banks.*

*Now in its 11th season, Clara's is a favorite for its waterfront location and proximity to local attractions such as the Lost Colony, Roanoke Island Festival Park and the Elizabeth II. Locals call this restaurant a favorite, returning time after time.*

## *Grilled Tuna Burgers*

3 lbs. chopped fresh tuna
3 T. olive oil
2 tsp. garlic
5 T. Dijon mustard
Salt & pepper to taste
½ c. teriyaki sauce
1 c. chicken stock
1 T. ginger
½ c. honey
1½ c. caramelized onions
8 hamburger buns

Mix tuna, oil, 1 tsp. garlic, 1 T. mustard, and salt and pepper. Form into 8 (6 oz.) patties.

Bring teriyaki, remaining garlic, chicken stock, ginger and honey to boil. Simmer until reduced to glaze. Stir in remaining mustard.

Grill tuna burgers. Warm onions, stir in glaze. Place each burger on bun and top with onion mixture.

# Coastal Cactus Southwestern Restaurant

Seagate North Shopping Center
3105 N. Croatan Hwy., MP 5½
Kill Devil Hills, North Carolina
Deby Curcio, Owner (252) 441-6600

Deby and her husband, Jim Curcio, saw a need for authentic Southwestern cuisine as visitors to the Outer Banks. Therefore in 1993 they decided to open Coastal Cactus because of Deby's love for cooking. She learned at an early age the art of cooking, the old fashioned way, in the kitchen.

Airy and bright, the interior of this ultra-casual eatery is decorated with sponge-painted walls in Mesa Jade and Melon. Colorful border lizards and spiced-up table tops is another Deby Curcio original.

The chips and tortillas are fried on premise and the salsas are homemade and bottled under the Coastal Cactus label for resale in their Southwestern gift shop and other locations in Virginia and North Carolina. Specialties here are the Sizzlin' ½-pound Fajita Fiesta, Ensaladas, Tequila-lime shrimp, chile rellenos, tacos and homemade margaritas. Selections come in every possible combination. There's a full menu of Mexican and American meals for "Little Amigo." The Coastal Cactus is open seven nights a week in season, serving dinner nightly and lunch Monday through Saturday. Prices are very reasonable.

## *Rockfisb Veracruz*

1 c. chopped onion
2 garlic cloves chopped
1 bay leaf
2 T. olive oil
½ c. sliced pimento-stuffed olives
½ c. dry white wine
¼ c. diced roasted green chiles
1 T. capers
Juice of one lime
2 large ripe tomatoes, seeded & chopped
1 T. chopped fresh oregano leaves, or
1 tsp. dried oregano
½ tsp. white pepper
½ tsp. black pepper
½ tsp. salt
2 lbs. fresh rockfish fillets

Sauté the chopped onion and garlic with the bay leaf in the oil over medium heat for 10 minutes. Add the olives and wine, cover and simmer for 15 minutes. Add the tomato, chiles, capers, lime juice, and spices; simmer for 5 minutes.

Add rockfish fillets to the pan with the sauce, cover and cook until just done, 5 to 15 minutes, depending on the thickness of your fillets. Serve hot, smothered with the sauce.

# Colington Café

*1029 Colington Road*
*Kill Devil Hills, North Carolina*
*Carlen & Kenneth Pearl, Owners (252) 480-1123*

*This popular restaurant is located only a mile off the bypass. Once you arrive, you'll feel as if you are stepping back in time with this Victorian style Café set high on a hill with its tranquil and unique setting amongst beautiful hundred year old live oaks.*

*The Pearls started out in a small sandwich shop on Colington Road and ten years later moved to the present location. They converted the Victorian style home into a restaurant. It's unique in both its setting and its menu. The Café has four different small dining rooms, each with a different touch.*

*The menu specializes in fresh local seafood with a gourmet touch. With Carlen's French heritage, the menu has a French emphasis. The recent addition of Chef Jeff Lane has brought in a new dimension of infusion cooking, with emphasis on fresh ingredients. The owners agree that they live in the best place for fresh ingredients---both seafood and produce. The menu also includes a wide selection of many beef, pork, chicken, and pasta dishes. All desserts are made on premises. This popular restaurant is a "must do".*

## Seafood Napoleon

*Shrimp and Scallops in a light cream sauce*

1 lb. large shrimp
1 lb. medium scallops
3 T. butter
1½ T. flour
½ small diced onion
5 to 6 T. heavy cream
⅛ c. sherry (cream) (you can substitute white wine, but flavor won't be as rich)

Sauté onion in butter for 1 minute. Put scallops and shrimp in. Keep heat medium-high. Cook about 2 minutes. Sprinkle flour in pan. Cook a few seconds--pour sherry in. Cook down for about 1 minute. Pour in cream. If sauce needs thickening, remove seafood with slotted spoon. Cook down 2-3 minutes. Put seafood back in. Serve with rice. Serves 4-5.

**Note:** Try not to use cooking sherry. A Taylor Cream sherry does great.

# Creekside Café

Highway 12, P.O. Box 368
Ocracoke, North Carolina
Christopher T. Styron, Owner (252) 928-3606

*Creekside Café welcomes you to enjoy a casual meal overlooking scenic Silver Lake Harbor. Dining on their covered porch from the second story is a wonderful vantage point. They offer friendly service serving brunch, lunch and dinner. Soups, salads, seafood and specialty sandwiches keep the locals coming back for more. So, stop by and join them! Save room for Key Lime pie or one of their other great homemade desserts.*

## Seafood Cakes

½ lb. lump crab meat
2 lbs. cooked popcorn shrimp
3 eggs
½ T. granulated garlic
2 tsp. yellow mustard
4 T. mayonnaise
1 small jar pimento
1 small onion diced
dash of parsley flakes

Mix all ingredients well and add bread crumbs to hold everything together. Make small cakes and fry at 350 degrees until golden brown. Enjoy!!

# Darrell's Restaurant

Highway 64
Manteo, North Carolina
Allan & Lorana Daniels, Owners (252) 473-5366

*This restaurant has been serving people since 1960 and has been a favorite family-style eatery for locals as well as tourists. You'll always feel welcome here with the down-home atmosphere. There's even a 932 lb. Blue Marlin mounted on the wall.*

*Menu items include fresh local seafood, steaks and chops, chicken, salads, appetizers, sandwiches. For the shuckers or peelers, there's a Steamed & Raw Seafood Bar. Two of my favorite soups are the Dare County Style Clam Chowder and the She Crab Soup. The fried oysters are the best in town. The desserts are wonderful, especially the hot fudge cake. Be sure and check the daily luncheon and dinner specials. A children's menu is also available. Darrell's is open year round for lunch and dinner but closed on Sundays.*

## She Crab Soup

2 qt. half & half
1 pt. milk
1 lb. backfin crab meat
1 lb. regular crabmeat
1 c. self-rising flour
½ stick margarine
1 tsp. chicken base
⅛ tsp. white pepper
¼ tsp. mace
¼ c. white cooking wine
Salt to taste
1 tsp. shrimp base

Heat half & half and milk in heavy saucepan under low heat. Make a paste by adding margarine and flour. Add mixture to heated milk. Add all seasonings. After heating thoroughly, add crab meat and wine.

# Duck Deli

1378 Duck Road (N.C. Hwy. 12)
Duck, North Carolina
Ron Forlano, Owner (252) 261-3354
Don Forlano, Owner, Chef

The Duck Deli was started 11 years ago as a barbecue restaurant specializing in pork, beef, and chicken barbecue, which are still their specialities. Philly cheese steaks, subs, sandwiches, salads, and a vast dessert menu of cobblers, brownies, and a frozen yogurt bar with plenty of toppings are available. A full breakfast menu includes everything from eggs, pancakes, and omelettes.

Six years ago they started smoking all different types of fish and shellfish, and as a result, Duck Deli became the home of the Carolina Blue Smoked Wildfish Company whose gourmet food products are sold all over the world and on the Outer Banks.

This is a very casual restaurant. You would feel comfortable dining in your bathing suit. Beer is also served. Open for breakfast, lunch and dinner.

## Smoked Tuna Salad

2 lbs. smoked tuna
½ c. sweet pickle relish
½ fresh lemon (juice with pulp)
1 c. celery, finely chopped
¼ c. onion, minced
Mayonnaise, added to the consistency you prefer.

Combine ingredients and serve as a tuna salad sandwich or on a bed of lettuce. Serves 6 to 8.

# Duck Seafood Buffet & Qwacker's Blind Duck Tavern

Duck, North Carolina

Darlene & Joe Morgan, Co-Managers (252) 261-3901

Wayne Hardesty, Chef Tavern (252) 261-8700

*Located in the heart of the now famous Duck Village, this sound side restaurant overlooks the beautiful Currituck Sound. Here, you can enjoy fabulous sunsets and delightful views through the wall of glass windows of this second floor dining room while enjoying the areas newest seafood buffet.*

*This is the place to dine if you love seafood. The 85 foot seafood and salad bar offers Oysters Rockefeller, mussel's, fried and steamed shrimp, clams, Alaskan crabs legs, scallops, crabmeat dishes, crab balls, chowders, prime rib, pork, barbecue, chicken, loads of vegetables and desserts and even solf-serve ice-cream. The list goes on and on.*

*If you prefer dining in a more casual atmosphere, Qwacker's Tavern on the first floor serves lunch, dinner and late night appetizers. Dinner specials are offered nightly and the views of the sound and sailing center are just as wonderful. Qwacker's features a large bar, 19 TV's, pool tables, shuffleboard. The outside deck is another lively and popular night- spot with live music entertainment nightly.*

*The restaurant and tavern is open seven days a week in season, The Seafood Buffet is served nightly in the upstairs dining area.*

## Qwacker's Tavern Crab Dip

8 oz. cream cheese
8 oz. sour cream
16 oz. crabmeat (Backfin)
1 T. lemon juice
1 tsp. Worcestershire sauce
½ tsp. dry mustard
½ tsp. chopped garlic
4 oz. grated cheddar cheese
½ oz. Half & Half
(milk can be used)

Soften cream cheese and mix all ingredients except crabmeat. With all ingredients mixed well, fold in crabmeat. Place in ovenproof dish and bake at 350 degrees for 20 minutes. Serve with French bread toast points.

# The Dunes Restaurant

U.S. Hwy 158, MP 16½
Nags Head, North Carolina

Rufus & Roxie Pritchard, Owners (252) 441-1600

*The Dunes Restaurant has been a Nags Head tradition since it first opened in 1983. In the 17 years since, it has been a meeting place for locals; a gathering place for far-flung, vacationing families; and always a warm and friendly dining institution for breakfast, lunch or dinner. Rufus and Roxie Pritchard and the entire Dunes staff make it their goal to give every visitor a great dining experience. In fact, "Southern Living" magazine in 1996 applauded how good The Dunes is, noting it's a "must place to stop on the Outer Banks . . ."*

*There's a lot of people who obviously agree because they come back, year after year, eager to make The Dunes part of their Outer Banks vacation. Friendly faces, generous portions, fresh food cooked to order, and a warm family atmosphere are trademarks of The Dunes Restaurant.*

*There's also a popular breakfast bar here during weekends in the off-season, daily in the summer, and nightly all-you-can-eat seafood feast with a 30-item salad bar.*

*Beulah Charity has been a cook for The Dunes for many, many years.*

## Beulah's Squash Casserole

1½ lbs. fresh squash
¼ tsp. pepper
½ c. chopped onion
⅛ tsp. salt
1 c. mayonnaise
2 T. butter or margarine, melted
1 c. Parmesan cheese
¾ c. French bread crumbs
2 eggs

Sauté squash and onion until tender. Drain well. Combine squash and onion with mayonnaise, cheese, eggs, and seasonings. Mix well and pour into casserole dish. Mix butter and bread crumbs until crumbly (add more crumbs if necessary). Sprinkle bread crumbs on top of squash. Bake 30 minutes at 350 degrees. This is the best. Serves 4-6.

# Elizabeth's Café & Winery

Chef Scarborough Faire Shoppes
Duck, North Carolina

Leonard Logan, Owner/Chef (252) 261-6145
Brad Price, Sous Chef

This quaint bistro nestled among the pines of Scarborough Faire has received accolades from their reviewers and guests as "one of the finest restaurants in the world for the pairing of food and wine." Elizabeth's has earned international acclaim as one of only 329 restaurants in the world to receive the Best of Award of Excellence by The Wine Spectator.

Elizabeth's is a cozy, warm and delightful place to dine. There's even a fireplace that's usually lit on cool evenings. Only a handful of restaurants in the world offer an a la carte menu and two prix fixe wine dinners (seven course meals with accompanying wines) nightly. The restaurant has a walk-in wine cellar and a tasting wine bar where you can try a wine before buying a bottle or case to go. Winemakers from around the world are sometimes featured here for special dinners.

Southern Living magazine said "Elizabeth's Café and Winery is Country French and Sensational. Its also some of the best food you're likely to find on the Outer Banks." The menu changes nightly and reflects the chef's daily purchases. Only at this restaurant will you enjoy some of the freshest ingredients of the day. A pastry chef creates different desserts daily.

*National Jazz acts entertain during the summer in the restaurants wine cellar. Elizabeth's is open for lunch and dinner seven days a week in season and on weekends in the off season. This café is so popular that you will want to make your reservations early. Reservations in season are a must.*

## *Scallop and Brie Bisque*

¾ gallon water
1 T. chicken/lobster base of each
2 ribs celery
1 onion
1 qt. cream
1 qt. half and half
½ lb. roux
1 kilo brie cheese
Scallops (use desired amount)

Sauté celery and onion, add water and chicken/lobster base, boil. Thicken chicken stock with roux, add heavy cream and half-half and simmer. Whisk in brie until dissolved. Season with salt and pepper. Poach scallops and add to soup. Serve immediately.

Serves 4 to 6

# *Etheridge Seafood Restaurant*

*Highway 158, MP 9½*
*Kill Devil Hills, North Carolina*
*"Capt. Will" Etheridge, Owner* (252) 441-2645

*Etheridge's has been in operation on the Outer Banks for 13 years. All this time it has been operated and supplied with fresh seafood by three generations of the Etheridge family.*

*Jennifer Etheridge is currently at the helm of the restaurant as first mate. She is the granddaughter of "Capt. Will," and the daughter of Irene Etheridge. Irene, "The Captain," runs a taunt ship assuring that nothing but the best seafood from the Etheridge Seafood Company is served at the restaurant.*

*Man your tables and knock the barnacles from your gullet at Etheridge's, as you go through their large selections of Outer Banks favorites; you won't come away disappointed.*

## *Mill Landing Seafood Eggroll*

½ c. lump crab meat
1 c. frozen spinach (drained)
½ c. medium green chili peppers
2 c. shredded Monterey Jack cheese
½ c. shrimp & scallops (chopped)
½ c. chopped black olives
2 c. medium salsa sauce
8 eggroll wrappers

Combine first 5 ingredients. Place 4 to 5 T. of filling slightly below the center of the wrapper. Fold the bottom side up to cover filling. Fold in side and roll the wrapper. Brush the top edges with water and seal. Heat the oil to 350 degrees in a 1-quart sauce pan, filled halfway up with vegetable or corn oil. Drop in eggroll and fry until golden brown (about 2 minutes). Serve with salsa sauce.

# Flying Fish Cafe

2003 S. Croatan Highway
158 Bypass, Milepost 10
Kill Devil Hills, North Carolina

George Price & John Xenakis, Owners (252) 441-6894
Billy Price, Chef

*The Flying Fish Cafe is a year round coastal restaurant that offers you a taste of American and Mediterranean inspired specialties. It is a dynamic value oriented restaurant that specializes in fresh local seafood, lean meat and poultry, plus unique vegetarian dishes. "From scratch" signature dishes comprise the majority of the menu. The Pastry chef will tempt you with desserts like the Chocolate Hurricane and the Grecian Urn. They also feature a wide choice of espresso and cappuccino drinks.*

*Not to be overlooked is the extensive wine list with over 40 wines available by the glass or bottle. Flying Fish Cafe for lunch or dinner--open year round, seven days a week. Reservations suggested.*

## Flying Fish Cafe Lobster Bisque

*For 2 gallons Lobster stock*

4 gallons water
5 lbs. lobster shells
4 large onions, quartered
6 carrots julienne
1 bunch celery diced
Salt & pepper to taste

Sear lobster shells in hot oil. Salt and pepper to taste. Add water, onions, celery and carrots. Reduce to one half.

Add and cook until soft:

2 c. diced pimentos
3 c. diced onions
3 c. diced celery

Thicken with 3 cups of water and 1 cup of corn starch, mixed together. Simmer for 20 minutes. Add 4 cups cooked lobster meat, diced. Parsley for garnish.

# *Frisco's Restaurant & Lounge*

*3833 N. Croatan Hwy., MP 4*
*Kitty Hawk, North Carolina*

*Mark & Cindy Dough, Owners* (252) 261-7833
*Jim Burch & Cliff Edmonds, Chefs*

*Frisco's is the oldest full service restaurant in Kitty Hawk, established in 1984, and one of the oldest restaurants on the Outer Banks.*

*It has a fun and lively atmosphere with beautiful aquariums, talking, trick trained parrots and "Frisco" a six-foot long iguana.*

*Frisco's is casual fine dining! Enjoy ocean views from the back porch while you dine on some of the best prime rib you'll find on the beach. Some of my favorite entrees are the seafood dishes, steaks, pasta, and authentic Cajun fare.*

*This is the place that you will find the friendliest bar on the beach with karaoke and live entertainment. This eatery is open year round, serving lunch and dinner.*

## *Charlie Brown Cheesecake*

2 T. butter softened
2 c. graham cracker crumbs
32 oz. cream cheese (2 lb.)
1 c. sugar
4 eggs
1 T. vanilla extract
1 T. lemon juice
2 c. chocolate chips (semi-sweet)
2 T. Gran Marnier (optional)
1 jar peanut butter (crunchy or smooth)

*Step 1.* Combine butter and cracker crumbs until well mixed (when pressed together mixture should hold shape). Pour into one 9-inch springform pan and press covering entire bottom.

*Step 2.* In a food processor, with regular blade, combine cream cheese and sugar until smooth. Pulse in eggs one at a time, again until smooth. Pulse in vanilla extract and lemon juice. Pour mixture into mixing bowl. Melt chocolate chips in double boiler or microwave. Blend into mixture slowly, mixing thoroughly until completely incorporated. Pour mixture into springform pan. Bake at 325 degrees for about 1 hour. Cool at room temperature for 30 minutes then refrigerate until set (overnight if possible).

*Step 3.* Once cheesecake is completely cooled, spread peanut butter on top (½ inch thick) and cool for 2 hours. Cut and serve. Serves up to 16 portions.

## Fishbones Raw Bar & Restaurant

1171 Duck Road
Duck, North Carolina

John Kotch, Owner (252) 255-3263
"Finely Ron" Davidson, Chef

This Bahamian-inspired eatery is located upstairs in the Scarborough Lane Shopping complex in Duck. Fishbones was Duck's first original Outer Banks-style Raw Bar, serving raw and steamed seafood. An always popular spot, this restaurant is always busy in season as the bar stretches the entire length of the dining area. It's a great place to meet friends and enjoy good food prepared by one of Outer Banks best chefs, Ron Davidson.

There's an extensive menu offering beef, chicken, pork and seafood prepared natural or with Caribbean sauces. Their Hatteras style Clam chowder won first place in the Outer Banks 1st Annual Chowder Cookoff!! Lunch entrees include sandwiches, soups, seafood baskets, burgers and specials of the day. For dinner, try the Seafood Alfredo made with a medley of tuna, shrimp and scallops tossed with linguine and homemade Alfredo sauce with parmesan cheese. Fishbones is open year-round for lunch and dinner.

### Fishbones Spicy Crab Dip

2 lbs. crab meat
2 lbs. cream cheese
2 cups heavy cream
½ cup culinary cream
9 oz. sherry
pinch of Old Bay
pinch of white pepper
1 T. Schreiher crab base
1 tsp. flaming ass (or hot sauce)

Place cream cheese in mixer with paddle and beat about 2 minutes. Scrape bowl while running mixer. Add heavy cream and sherry. Turn off and scrape bowl. Turn on low and add picked crab meat, Old Bay and white pepper. Scrape into container. Refrigerate.

# The Full Moon Cafe

The Waterfront Shops
207 Queen Elizabeth Street
Manteo, North Carolina
Sharon Enoch & Paul Charron, Chef-Owners (252) 473-6666

Nestled in the heart of downtown Manteo, overlooking Shallowbag Bay lies a legendary Cafe where the view is exceptional and the food is sublime. Amidst the quaint seaside town The Full Moon Cafe opened its doors in the fall of 1995 to the rave reviews of locals and tourists. In an area known for outstanding seafood, the chef/owners of the cafe brought their own special twist to the local cuisine adding international sauces and culinary favorites from around the world. Seafood, fresh and intriguing sauces, imaginative soups, huge salads, tempting sandwiches and the largest selection of vegetarian entrees in the area dot this interesting and well-balanced menu.

Sharon and Paul invite everyone to come to Manteo and enjoy a wonderful afternoon of shopping, strolling, bird watching, and visiting one of North Carolina's premiere historic sites: Festival Park and the Elizabeth II. Take a break during the day to relax in their jewel of a dining room, enjoy great food, and savor one of the best views the Outer Banks has to offer. The Full Moon Cafe is open year round, but the hours are seasonal so call ahead to reserve a table.

The following recipe for Mushroom Gorgonzola soup was developed by Sharon as many recipes were and still are: she looks around the kitchen, sees what is handy and concocts. It is said that baking is a science, but true cooking comes from the heart. It is in this spirit that this recipe is tendered..experiment and add, substitute and augment, stir, taste and add some more. Nothing is written in stone. However, Sharon has one rule: She always starts with an onion....

## *Mushroom Gorgonzola Soup*

1 medium onion
2 stalks celery
2 T. butter
1 T. chicken or vegetable base
1 tsp. dill (dried)
1 lb. mushrooms (white, portobella or shiitake: the greater the variety, the greater the complexity)
1 qt. heavy cream or milk
1 qt. water
2 T. flour or yellow cornmeal
Salt & pepper
4 oz. gorgonzola cheese

Sauté the onions and celery until translucent. Add sliced mushrooms and sauté until limp. Add the flour or cornmeal, base and dill, and sauté for 5 minutes. Add the water, then the milk or cream, and reduce heat. Do not boil at this point or the soup will curdle. Crumble the gorgonzola and add, leaving enough time before serving for the cheese to melt. At this point you could also add some drained frozen spinach, basil or corn. Again, the basics of soup making are sautéing veggies and adding stock, so create away and let your imagination run wild.

# George's Junction

2806 Virginia Dare Trail (Beach Road), MP 11
Nags Head, North Carolina

Jerry Dowless, Manager (252) 441-0606
Jeff Price, Executive Chef

*You'll recognize this large restaurant by the white and gold domes with the giant windmill on the front of the building, giving it the appearance of a mosque in Holland. The decor inside is simple with a Casablanca atmosphere.*

*George's Junction is known for having the largest Seafood & Crab Leg Buffet on the beach with over 70 items. Beef, chicken and pasta entrees are served as well as soups and appetizers, fresh vegetables, and a 30-item fruit and salad bar. The seafood au gratin is filled with scallops and shrimp in a rich sauce and just happens to be one of my favorites. The desserts are homemade, so save room for them.*

*There is a limited menu available if someone chooses not to have the buffet, and special children's prices are available. A large lounge with a full bar is offered.*

## Blackened Tuna

4 to 6 3 oz. tuna fillets
1½ tsp. garlic powder
2 tsp. salt
1 tsp. cayenne pepper
1 tsp. dried thyme
½ tsp. ground white pepper
1 tsp. dried crushed basil
2½ tsp. paprika
1 c. olive oil
1 c. white wine
½ c. chopped green onions

Heat iron skillet on high for 5-6 minutes. Mix all seasonings in bowl. Dip tuna fillets in olive oil and white wine mixture, then coat with seasonings. Place tuna fillets in hot skillet 2-3 minutes on each side. Garnish with chopped green onion tops.

# Goombay's Grill & Raw Bar

1608 N. Virginia Dare Trail, MP 7
Kill Devil Hills, North Carolina
John Kirchmmier, Owner (252) 441-6001
Bruce W. Crouch, Chef

*Known on the Outer Banks as a fun place for good food, drinks, and just a great place to hang out. Locals love this place. The ambiance is upbeat and casual with bright and colorful surroundings. A wall-size tropical mural covers one wall of the dining area. The horseshoe-shaped bar is a great place to have a drink and try some of the great appetizers. A raw bar is open until late serving steamed shrimp, oysters and many other favorites.*

*Goombay's serves great local seafood with a Caribbean eclectic influence. A variety of foods anywhere from Asian to Cajun to Continental can be found here. For lunch, try one of the specials of the day or a great hamburger, sandwiches or coconut shrimp. Open for lunch and dinner year round.*

## Goombay's West Indian Curried Chicken

8 boneless, skinless chicken breast halves
1 c. raisins
2 to 3 bananas, peeled and sliced
*Sauce*
1 qt. heavy cream
5 oz. cream of coconut (Coco Lopez or other)
1 T. curry powder
1 T. allspice
1 T. ground coriander
1 T. granulated garlic (garlic powder)
1 T. cayenne pepper
2 T. salt

Pound chicken breasts until ¼ in. thick. Make sauce by melting cream of coconut in a bowl and adding dry ingredients; mix thoroughly. Whip in cream until smooth. Heat 1 or 2 T. of clarified butter or oil in sauté pan over medium-high heat. When just smoking, add chicken breasts. (May need 2 batches, depending on pan size.) Sauté breasts for 2 or 3 minutes; turn and sauté for an additional 2 minutes. Add raisins and bananas. Add sauce and cook for an additional 2 or 3 minutes or until chicken is done. Plate chicken and reduce sauce for another minute or so until desired consistency is obtained. Pour sauce equally over breasts and garnish with a tablespoon of Major Grey's Chutney and flaked coconut. Serves 4 to 8.

# *Great Dane Deli & Wrong Dog Cafe*

*120 E. Kitty Hawk Road*
*Kitty Hawk, North Carolina*

*Dawn Didriksen & Glenn Schumacher, Owners (252) 255-3263*
*(wife and husband)*
*Michael DeStefano, Chef*

*The Great Dane Deli & Wrong Dog Cafe may be a funny name for a restaurant, but owners Dawn Didriksen and Glenn Schumacher are very serious about their Kitty Hawk eatery. From the 45 different lunch sandwiches to the dinner menu featuring Retro Regional American cuisine, to the spacing between the tables in the comfortable dining room, Dawn and Glenn pay attention to the details of their establishment.*

*The niche they are filling is between the beach hangout type places and the white tablecloth restaurants spaced around the Outer Banks. The Great Dane Deli & Wrong Dog Cafe offers plenty of food at reasonable prices in a quiet, comfortable and casual atmosphere. With a full service bar (8 tap beers) and a nice selection of wines by the glass and bottle, they have something for just about everyone.*

## *Shrimp Ala Peppernata*

*This dish combines the zesty flavor of pepper vinegar with the sweetness of heavy whipping cream to create a unique and light alternative to the more traditional shrimp alfredo.*

8 shrimp, peeled and deveined
6 oz. cheese tortellini, cooked
3 oz. pepper vinegar
2 oz. heavy whipping cream
3 banana pepper rings
5 roasted pepper slices
1 tsp. garlic
2 oz. fresh herb mixture (or pesto)

Sauté shrimp with garlic and fresh herb mixture. Remove shrimp and deglaze pan with pepper vinegar. Reduce liquid and add pepper rings and roasted pepper strips. Return shrimp to pan, add heavy cream and bring to quick boil. Turn heat off and add cooked tortellini, stir and serve.

# Grouper's
# Grill & Wine Bar

790-G Ocean Trail, TimBuckII Shopping Village
Corolla, North Carolina

Tommy Karole, Owner (252) 453-4077
Rob McConnell, Executive Chef

This is one of the most outstanding restaurants on the Outer Bank's serving up an array of diverse and enticing entrees created in an atmosphere of elegance. Tommy Karole and Chef Rob McConnell emphasize teamwork to produce a menu that is diverse and appealing. The menu changes seasonally to reflect the freshest ingredients available. Their specialties include local seafood served with an international twist, Black Angus beef, Lean Generation pork, and Free Range chicken. Unusual spices and sauces give the food here a flavor all its own.

Appetizers include temptations such as tuna sashimi served with pickled cucumber salad fresh vegetables sushi rolls and a green wasabi aiolo, marinated Portabella mushroom, freshly made soups, and salads. Entrée's like seafood puff pastry with shrimp and sea scallops served in a puff pastry shell with French green beans, chive mashed potatoes and a sherry shrimp bisque sauce or blackened grouper with succotash and jalapeno beurre blanc are exquisite. Entrees come with a choice of gourmet soup or salad. All the breads, sauces, dressings, and desserts are made from scratch. The desserts are absolutely wonderful and are prepared daily on the premises by their pastry chef.

Grouper's offers more than 150 wines from which to choose and a wide variety of beers are also served at the huge wine bar. Open for lunch and dinner during summer season. Reservations accepted

## *Grilled Romaine*

2 medium heads of Romaine lettuce
4 tablespoons olive oil
Salt and Pepper
4 Roma tomatoes halved
1 red onion thinly sliced into rings
1 cup crumbled Feta cheese

1. Cut Romaine in half lengthwise leaving stalk in tact to hold the leaves together.
2. Coat each half of Romaine with olive oil and salt and pepper to taste.
3. Place lettuce flat side down on grill for 1 to 1 ½ minutes then turn and cook for an additional minute. Lettuce should be golden brown and slightly wilted when finished.
4. Place lettuce cut side up on large salad plate, top with red onion, Feta cheese and balsamic vinaigrette, garnish with tomato halves and serve. Serves 4

## *Balsamic Shallot Vinaigrette*

1 cup Balsamic vinegar
2 medium shallots sliced
1 egg yolk (optional)
1 ½ cups olive oil or salad oil

1. In a non-stick sauce pan add vinegar and shallots and reduce until mixture is ¾ of the original amount. The reduction should be the consistency of syrup. Set mixture aside to cool.
2. Once reduction is completely cooled add egg yolk, mix very slowly with electric mixer. Continue mixing while slowly adding the oil. If mixture should begin to get pasty thin with water. Season with salt and pepper.

## Henry's Beef and Seafood

Hwy. 158 Bypass, MP 5
Kill Devil Hills, North Carolina
Henry & Linda Ezzell, Owners (252) 261-2025

*Henry's is a great place for families to dine in a casual atmosphere. Open seven days a week year round serving breakfast, lunch and dinner with specials offered daily. Senior citizens menus are also available. This is a favorite restaurant for locals. Menu choices feature basic American fare specializing in broiled or fried seafood, chicken, pasta, and prime rib or steaks.*

*In business here for 10 years, the Ezzells offer great food at a reasonable price. A separate non-smoking room is available, all ABC permits.*

### Brownie Pie

1½ lbs. butter or oleo
12 oz. unsweetened chocolate
12 eggs
6 c. sugar
4 T. vanilla
3 c. sifted self-rising flour

Melt butter and chocolate, add eggs and stir till smooth. Add sugar, vanilla, and flour. Whisk till well blended and pour into 9-inch pans. Bake at 350 degrees for 22-25 minutes. Serve hot with or without vanilla ice cream. Makes four 9-inch pies.

# *Herrons Deli and Restaurant*

*1202 Duck Road*

*Duck, North Carolina*

*Rick and Kathy Herron, Owners* (252) 261-3224

*This ultra-casual eatery is located in the heart of Duck with easy excess and plenty of parking. Herron's has become one of the most popular breakfast and lunch places in Duck. Pancakes, eggs, sausage, french toast, omelettes, biscuits, sausage and bacon and anything else you could desire is on the breakfast menu.*

*Lunch specials are posted daily and include such local favorites as crab cakes, lasagna, meat loaf, burgers, sandwiches, soups, salads. Desserts include pies, cake, and other specials of the day. Prices are very reasonable here. For dinner, choose fresh local seafood, beef, chicken, or one of the nightly specials.*

*Open year-round for breakfast, lunch. Dinner is offered nightly here in season. Closed on Sundays.*

## *Crab Cakes*

1 lb. lump crab meat
2 T. chopped fine, green onion
1/8 tsp. black pepper
1 T. parsley
½ cup bread crumbs
1 egg
¼ cup mayonnaise
1/3 cup milk
Whip egg, mayonnaise, milk together

Combine together all of the above and then fold in crab meat
Pan fry in butter 2 ½ minutes per side. Serves 6

# Howard's Pub & Raw Bar Restaurant

N.C. Hwy. 12, P.O. Box 670
Ocracoke, North Carolina
Buffy & Ann Warner, Owners (252) 928-4441

Howard's Pub & Raw Bar Restaurant is the only raw bar on Ocracoke Island. A fun place with great local flavor, no trip to Ocracoke would be complete without a visit to Howard's Pub, home of the famous "Ocracoke Oyster Shooter." You can sit out on the screened-in porch that stretches the entire length of the restaurant or sit inside at one of the wooden tables. Inside you can dance to live music, watch TV or play games; and if you are not into having fun, you can just sit around and watch everyone else having fun.

Howard's boasts a huge beer and wine list. This includes over 214 domestic and imported beers. Lunch and dinner items include subs, burgers, sandwiches, snow crab legs, fried shrimp, soups and salads, munchies, chicken and seafood platters.

Buffy Warner is very modest; and if you ask him to boast a little about his restaurant, he will say, "We do make a n umber of items here by hand or from scratch. For example, our chili—but everyone has their own chili recipe; our Italian dressing for subs and salads—but again, not many people need a recipe for salad dressing; our french fries—but that just requires using the right Idaho potatoes and cutting them by hand; our burgers, everybody makes burgers—we use 81% lean beef and shape each one by hand. We are dedicated to using only fresh local vegetables and products when available."

Buffy, I think you just said all that needs to be said! Howard's is open 365½ days a year, from lunchtime until the owls go to bed. The Warners work hard to make your visit to Ocracoke Island a memorable one. Stop in and give them an "Atta Boy" for a job well done.

## *Ocracoke Oyster Shooter*

2 to 3 oz. your favorite beer
1 freshly shucked oyster
Dash of Texas Pete, Tabasco sauce,
or your preferred hot sauce

Put freshly shucked oyster in a small glass. Add beer. Top with dash of hot sauce and enjoy. Typically, the shooter is consumed in one swallow (although some people prefer to hold the oyster in their mouth a bit to savor), and one or two aren't normally near enough! Real beer lovers say, "The beer helps the oyster go down," but the real oyster lovers say, "The oyster helps the beer go down!"

# *Hurricane Mo's*

*Restaurant & Raw Bar*
*Pirates' Cove, Manteo-Nags Head Causeway*
*Nags Head, North Carolina*

*Jeff and Maureen Ashworth, Owners* *(252) 473-2266*
*Greg Rector, Executive Chef*

*You'll find this great casual restaurant perched atop the ship's store of Pirate's Cove Marina on Roanoke Island. Floor-to-ceiling windows offer magnificent water views of the sound and causeway and to the east, Pirate's Cove charter fleet. A covered deck wraps around the restaurant for those who want to dine and relax outdoors or just want to watch the returning Gulfstream Fleet.*

*Hurricane Mo's serves traditional entrees such as broiled, fried and steamed seafood platters, New York strip, filet mignon, crab cakes, salads and sandwiches, appetizers. There is a full bar separate from the dining area. A children's menu is available. Lunch and Dinner served daily in season*

## *Caribbean Cream of Tomato Avocado Soup*

Chicken stock
1 bunch of Celantro leaves and Coriander stems (minced)
Crushed and pureed tomatoes
White Roux
Pureed Haas avocados
3 minced Scots bonnet peppers
4 bulbs of fresh minced garlic
8 cubed avocados
8 cubed tomatoes

In 2 qt. pot, bring stock to boil and add minced Scots bonnet peppers, fresh minced garlic, celantro leaves and coriander stems (minced). Salt to taste. Thicken with white Roux to desired consistency. Add pureed avocados and pureed crushed tomatoes. If too thick add chicken stock to loosen. After soup is done, add cubed tomatoes, cubed avocados. Check and adjust seasoning accordingly. (*A native soup of the Caribbean)* Yield—approximately 30 servings.

# *Island Inn Restaurant*

*Lighthouse Road, Ocracoke Village*
*Ocracoke, North Carolina*
*Robert & Claudia Toubey, Owners (252) 928-4351*

*The Island Inn was built in 1901 and is listed with the National Register of Historic places. In 1950 the east wing was added with a dining room on the first floor. Today the main dining room and side porch are furnished in a traditional country style, with nautical touches throughout. The family owned and operated restaurant at the Island Inn is one of the oldest buildings on Ocracoke Island.*

*Breakfast, lunch and dinner are served daily, except in midwinter. The breakfast menu includes the standard, but the chef adds an extra touch with his Shrimp, Oyster or Crab omelet. For dinner, local fried, broiled seafood and shellfish are served. Other entrees include shrimp and chicken parmesan, beef, pork, lamb, and pasta dishes. Vegetarian dishes are also available. All the breads and soups are made daily along with the delicious homemade pies and cakes. The Island Inn Fishcakes are a favorite among guests. They use red chum (channel bass) for fishcakes, but they like to use grayling drum the best. If drum is unavailable, you may use bluefish, trout, flounder or a combination. Fishcakes are served with tartar sauce, green chile cheese grits, and coleslaw.*

## *Island Inn Fishcakes*

1½ lbs. fish fillets, skinned & boned
1 to 1½ lbs. potatoes, peeled & diced
  into ⅓-in. cubes
1 small onion, chopped fine
¼ c. mayonnaise
2 T. Dijon mustard
1 T. Worcestershire sauce
1 T. fresh lemon juice
2 T. chopped cooked bacon
¼ tsp. cayenne pepper
½ tsp. lemon pepper
Dash of salt
Dry bread crumbs

Poach fish in water until cooked well. Drain, flake into large bowl. Boil potatoes in water until just fork tender, not mushy. Drain well. Add to fish. Add remaining ingredients except bread crumbs. Mix together lightly. Use your hands to pat mixture in cakes, then roll cakes in bread crumbs to coat. At this point the fishcakes can be pan sautéed, fried lightly in oil, or frozen for a future date. Makes approximately 12 to 15 3 oz. cakes.

# Jolly Roger Restaurant

1836 N. Virginia Dare Trail (Beach Road), MP 6¾
Kill Devil Hills, North Carolina
Carol Ann Angelos, Owner (252) 441-6530
Danny Klubowicz, Chef-C.E.C., A.C.F.

*This cozy white cottage with the big glass bubble is known as the "Jolly Roger." It sits across the road from the ocean and has been catering to locals and tourists since 1972. It's a comfortable, casual place where you just might run into someone you least expect to see.*

*Guests enjoy great Italian food, good old-fashioned breakfasts, diner type lunches and fresh seafood, steaks, pasta and prime rib, featured at dinner. There is entertainment and trivia games nightly in the lounge and a full late night menu until 1 a.m. A new addition has been added expanding the bar area to include a piano bar and dance floor. Be sure and say 'Hi' to Carol Ann, she's there most of the time.*

## Stuffed Flounder

2 ea. 5 to 7 oz. flounder fillets
3 oz. butter
Juice of 1 lemon
1 T. roasted garlic pepper
1 oz. white wine
Salt and pepper to taste
2 oz. lump crabmeat
2 oz. small shrimp, peeled
1 oz. mayonnaise
1 oz. bread crumbs
6 oz. heavy cream
2 oz. tomato sauce
1 tsp. each, chopped basil & parsley

To make stuffing: Combine the crabmeat, shrimp, mayonnaise, and bread crumbs.

To make sauce: Mix together the heavy cream, tomato sauce, basil and parsley. Heat and reduce until thickened.

Place 1 of the flounder fillets, skin side down on a greased sizzle plate. Place the filling in the center of the fillet. Cut a slit down the center of the other fillet, being careful not to cut so far as to separate the fillet. Place this fillet over the top of the stuffing and spread apart to partly expose the stuffing. Sprinkle the lemon juice, white wine, salt and pepper, and roasted garlic pepper seasoning over the stuffed flounder. Bake in a preheated 350-degree oven for 15-20 minutes. Remove from oven, top with the sauce and serve. Be sure to remind everyone that the platter is hot!

# Keeper's Galley Restaurant

U.S. Hwy. 158, MP 4
Kitty Hawk, North Carolina
Rufus & Roxie Pritchard, Owners (252) 261-4000

*In the days when the Outer Banks was earning a reputation as the "Graveyard of the Atlantic," sailing vessels were constantly being dashed upon our shores. To protect seafarers and their cargo, the United States Life Station Service placed Life Saving Stations every seven miles along the Outer Banks. These stations were manned by a crew of eight; seven crew and their leader, the Keeper.*

*Activity was limited for the crew and Keeper, so dining became the focus for relaxation. The owners take the name, Keeper's Galley, seriously and have built a restaurant that lives up to that tradition. Rufus and Roxie Pritchard and the entire staff of Keeper's Galley make all visitors comfortable with a warm, relaxed atmosphere and generous portions for breakfast, lunch and dinner. This family restaurant specializes in hearty meals, good service, and plenty of home cooking in an atmosphere that is steeped in Outer Banks' tradition. Dinner entrees change daily but include such regular offerings as prime rib, chicken, a surf and turf platter, crab cakes, and pasta.*

## Crabmeat Casserole

½ c. diced onions
½ c. chopped mushrooms
2 c. crabmeat
2 hard boiled eggs (chopped)
¾ c. mayonnaise
1 T. prepared mustard
1 T. lemon juice
1 tsp. Worcestershire sauce
2 T. dry vermouth
Dash cayenne
½ tsp. ea. salt & pepper
2 c. soft bread crumbs (or cornflakes)
½ c. melted butter or margarine

Sauté onions and mustard in small amount of oil. Combine crabmeat, onion, mushrooms and eggs in 1½-quart casserole dish. Mix mayonnaise, mustard, lemon juice, Worcestershire sauce, dry vermouth, cayenne, salt and pepper. Add to crabmeat mixture. Top with bread crumbs which have been mixed with melted butter. Bake at 350 degrees for 25-30 minutes. Bread crumbs may be topped with grated cheese. Serves 4.

# Kelly's

Outer Banks Restaurant & Tavern
US Hwy. 158 Bypass, MP 10
Nags Head, North Carolina

Mike Kelly, Owner (252) 441-4116
Wesley Stepp, Executive Chef

*Kelly's is one of the most popular restaurants on the Outer Banks and considered to be a tradition among many visitors that return year after year. Owner Mike Kelly is always present greeting guests and giving special attention to every detail of service. When you visit Kelly's, you'll dine amongst the largest collection of Outer Banks' memorabilia and artifacts to be found anywhere. This large upscale restaurant is an extremely busy place in season. Open year round, dinner is served nightly. The menu offers the freshest selections from the sea as well as tender beef, veal and delicate pasta. Homemade breads, including sweet potato biscuits, are served with all meals.*

*The raw bar offers oysters, clams, crab legs, and shrimp. Great live entertainment can be found at Kelly Tavern nightly starting at 10 p.m. when it becomes a fun-loving party place.*

## Flounder Piccata

6 oz. flounder fillet (skin on or off)
2 oz. drawn butter
1 T. capers
Juice of ½ lemon
½ lemon thinly sliced
2 T. white wine
Flour
2 eggs whipped
½ tsp. garlic
Salt & pepper
Parmesan cheese

Pat flounder fillet dry and dredge in plain flour, then add in whipped eggs to coat fish. (Dispose of excess egg coating.) Heat butter in sauté pan, preferably with wooden or non-burning handle. Lay fish in hot butter, skin side down, let pan fry for 2-3 minutes, making sure fish does not stick. Turn fish, add capers, lemon juice, wine, garlic, and salt and pepper to taste. Garnish the fish with slices of lemon and Parmesan cheese. Place whole pan in 350-degree preheated oven for 5 minutes or until fish is flaky and golden brown. Pour drippings on fish and serve with favorite rice or pasta.

# Kitty Hawk Pier Restaurant

Virginia Dare Trail, N.C. Hwy. 12 MP 1
Kitty Hawk, North Carolina
Luke Jacobs, Business owner (252) 261-3151

This has to be one of the most popular places on the beach for breakfast. Spectacular views from every seat allow patrons to get caught up in the rhythm of the waves. You will find just about anything on the breakfast menu that you desire, including eggs, omelettes, sausage, bacon, french toast, pancakes, grits and biscuits.

This is a great, laid-back place to enjoy lunch or dinner with friends and family. Locals know this is the place to come for good food and great prices. There's always lunch and dinner specials that include such favorites as ham and cabbage, fried chicken, trout, meat loaf, turkey and shrimp. All dinner specials come with a choice of two sides: coleslaw, vegetables in season, beans, beets, bush puppies and rolls.

Desserts are homemade and include such favorites as bread pudding, strawberry shortcake, pies and cobblers. A children's menu is available for the little crumb snatchers. The restaurant is open from April through November serving breakfast, lunch and dinner daily.

## Peach Cobbler

1 yellow cake mix
2 cans peach pie filling
¼ tsp. nutmeg
1 tsp. cinnamon
1 lemon (juice of)
1 tsp. vanilla flavoring
1 stick of butter (melted) or amount suitable for you

Combine in bowl peach pie filling, nutmeg, cinnamon, lemon juice, vanilla. Pour mixture into a lightly greased 9 x 13 inch baking pan. Sprinkle dry cake mix over peach mixture. Drizzle melted butter over top of cake mix. Bake in 350 degree oven for 30 to 45 minutes or until cake is golden brown on top. Makes about 4 to 8 servings.

## *Leo's Deli and Café*

*55 Sunset Boulevard*
*Timbuck II, Corolla, North Carolina*
*Leo Gavalas & Josh Mackellar, Owners (252) 453-6777*
*Josh Mackellar, Head Chef*

*Leo's is open year round, with a sit down or carry out menu for breakfast, lunch or dinner. The food is served at hungry man portions, with a friendly "You-all come back and see us, hear" attitude. The menu is vast, with emphasis on their 8 oz. 100-percent all beef burgers. Breakfast lovers will just go crazy over their Greek omelet.*

### *Greek Omelet*

3 eggs, beaten until light and fluffy (almost to a peak)
Onions, diced
Tomatoes, diced
Green peppers, diced
Feta cheese, crumbled
Greek olives
Butter

Heat a non-stick frying pan over medium-high heat. Add 1 T. butter and diced vegetables, sauté for about 15 seconds. Add the beaten eggs, top with feta cheese and olives. Cook until lightly browned on bottom. Fold into an omelet and slide onto a serving plate. My mouth is watering just thinking about it.

# Mako Mike's

1630 N. Croatan Hwy., Route 158, MP 7
Kill Devil Hills, North Carolina

Mac Ritter, Executive Chef (252) 480-1919

It's easy to spot this luscious-colored restaurant with its gigantic carved shark on the front and lots of shark tails protruding out of the lawn. It's even more decorative inside with sharks peering at diners from almost every angle of the unique three-level dining area. There's even a 200-gallon aquarium in the waiting area.

It's the good food, moderate prices, and friendly staff that keep diners returning to this establishment. Traditional and Cajun flavored food, fresh local seafood, salads, pastas, wood-oven pizza, meat dishes, and daily specials are available. Don't forget to visit their gift shop or have a cocktail in the Enchanted Octopus Lounge. Of all of the delicious homemade desserts, a favorite of the customer's is the Chocolate Passion Cake.

## Chocolate Passion Cake

16 oz. semi-sweet chocolate chips
8 oz. butter, salted
1 c. cocoa powder
7 eggs
1½ c. sugar
1 c. walnuts or pecans
Softened butter & flour
for 10" springform pan

Rub inside of springform pan with butter and lightly coat with flour; tap out excess flour. Wrap outside of springform pan with foil. Melt chocolate and butter in metal bowl over double-boiler and stir until smooth. Add cocoa powder and stir mixture with a whisk until blended; approximately 5 minutes. Set mixture aside.

In another metal bowl, combine eggs and sugar, and warm over double-boiler. Stir constantly until mixture is 110 degrees or lukewarm (2-3 minutes). Pour mixture into mixing bowl of electric mixer and using the whisk attachment, whip until tripled in volume. Fold this mixture into chocolate mixture along with the nuts using a rubber spatula (do not mix). Pour mixture into springform pan. Place springform pan into another pan which has ½ inch of hot water. Bake for 40-45 minutes. Remove from oven and cool. Remove springform pan from cake. Slice and serve with sweetened whipped cream.

# Millers Seafood & Steak House

1520 S. Virginia Dare Trail (Beach Rd.), MP 9½
Nags Head, North Carolina
Eddie & Lou Miller, Owners (252) 441-7674
Brian Miller, Food & Beverage

*Millers Seafood & Steak House is a family owned and operated restaurant. Sensational seafood at family prices has kept them in business for over 21 years. A large menu is available with "All You Can Eat" items such as clam strips, ocean trout, and popcorn shrimp; specializing in fresh seafood and steaks, an oyster and raw bar, and your favorite mixed beverages. Appetizers, salads, and sandwiches are also available.*

*Millers is still serving their famous 99-cent breakfast after all these years. Open for breakfast and dinner from March to late fall. Be sure and visit their other location: Millers Waterfront Restaurant overlooking Roanoke Sound on the bypass at Milepost 16 in Nags Head. All the Millers, Eddie, Lou, Brian, Beth, Whitney, Bryan W. and Alexandra hope you will enjoy this recipe.*

## Outer Banks Stuffed Flounder

½ c. mayonnaise
¼ c. Dijon mustard
1 lb. fresh lump crabmeat
pinch lemon pepper
pinch cayenne pepper
pinch garlic salt
2 T. bread crumbs
12 5 oz. skinless boneless flounder fillets

Mix mayonnaise, mustard, lemon pepper, cayenne pepper, garlic salt and bread crumbs in mixing bowl; add crabmeat (be sure to remove any shell) and gently fold into mixture.

Slice 6 of the flounder fillets in half; lay the other 6 flounder fillets about 2 inches apart from each other on a buttered baking pan.

Spoon 3 oz. crab mix on top of flounder fillets; place the sliced fillets on the top of the stuffed fillets and brush lightly with melted butter. Broil in oven approximately 15 minutes. Yields 6 servings.

# Millie's

2008 S. Virginia Dare Trail (Beach Rd.) MP 9.5
Kill Devil Hills, North Carolina
Paul and Lisa Keevil, Owners (252) 480-3463

In 1996, the Keevil's opened Millie's on the Outer Banks of North Carolina after establishing a very successful Millie's in the historic area of Church Hill in Richmond, Virginia. Their interest in vintage diners led them to purchase a 1939 Kullman diner in Richmond. Once restored to its' former glory, it was moved to North Carolina and will soon be listed as the sixth diner in the country on the National Register of Historic Buildings.

Over the years, Millie's has become recognized for adventurous, creative food and artful presentation. There is no set "influence"--there are many and they are ever-changing. The carefully selected wine list also changes often and features many lesser-known varietals. They are also known for having the best jukebox around, with classic individual Seeburgs at each booth and on the counter. The eclectic menus, music and casual service combine to set Millie's apart from the rest of the pack.

The dinner menu offers both light fare or full blown entrees such as Parmesan crusted tuna with sage, basil and lemon butter. Seafood specials are available nightly. Millie's has received regional and national press coverage including features in Bon Appetit, Gourmet, Travel & Leisure, Southern Living, the Los Angeles Times, the New York Times. Food at this restaurant is creative and delicious.

Open for breakfast, lunch, dinner.

## White Cheddar and Ale Soup with Sausage Crostini

5 T. butter
¾ cup plus 2 tablespoons minced shallots
2 garlic cloves, minced
5 tablespoons all purpose flour
2 cups (or more) chicken stock
  or canned low-salt broth
1 cup pale ale
1 ½ cups grated white cheddar cheese
½ cup whipping cream
3 ounces fully cooked smoked sausage (such as Kielbasa
  or surry sausage), cut into ¼-inch dice
1 tomato, peeled, seeded, chopped
2 T. olive oil
1 T. balsamic vinegar
1 T. minced fresh basil
8 ½-inch-thick baguette bread slices, toasted

Melt butter in heavy large saucepan over medium heat. Add ¾ cup shallots and garlic; sauté until tender, about 6 minutes. Add flour; stir 4 minutes (do not brown). Gradually whisk in 2 cups stock and ale. Increase heat; bring to boil, whisking constantly. Reduce heat and simmer until slightly thickened, about 8 minutes. Add cheese by handfuls, whisking until melted and smooth. Add cream; stir to heat through. Season with salt and pepper. (*can be made 1 day ahead. Cover and chill. Rewarm over low heat, thinning with more stock if necessary.)*

Combine sausage, tomato, oil, vinegar, basil and 2 tablespoons shallots in small bowl. Season with salt and pepper. Spoon sausage mixture onto toasts.

Serve soup with Crostini.

# Miriam's

Monteray Plaza
Corolla, North Carolina

Ann Runnels, Owner and Chef (252) 453-2571

*Ann Runnels has had a great response since she opened this New American Cuisine restaurant in July of 1996. Miriam's offers a comfortable and casual atmosphere with contemporary geometric décor and classy white walls.*

*Some favorite signature dishes offered at Miriam's are brown sugar and mustard marinated sliced pork tenderloin served with braised red cabbage slaw and cheddar scallion mashed potatoes or try the five cheese seafood lasagna. Other favorites include cornflake crusted jumbo lump crab cakes, shellfish stew in a saffron citrus broth, and a almond dipped fried seafood platter. A different pasta dish is featured nightly as are chicken, beef and fresh fish specials.*

*An assortment of homemade desserts are available as are a full beer and wine menu. Miriam's is also a full service caterer either on or off premise. A children's menu is available. Open May through late fall for dinner. Reservations are encouraged.*

## Miriam's Chilled Cucumber and Dill Soup

4 large cucumbers (peeled and seeded)
1 ½ gallon buttermilk
3 T. fresh chopped dill
1 lemon (juice of)
1 lime (juice of)
1 T. Balsamic vinegar
1 T. Worcestershire Sauce
1 ½ T. cracked black pepper
Salt to taste

Cut cucumbers into 1 inch pieces and chop in food processor—not too fine—small chunky style. Stir into buttermilk with all other ingredients, let sit over-night. Taste!
Serve in chilled bowls and garnish with lobster or shrimp and fresh dill sprig. Very refreshing. Enjoy! **Note:** Heavy cream and or more buttermilk can be added for a milder and thinner soup.

# Mulligan's Oceanfront Grille

2519 S. Virginia Dare Trail (Beach Road), MP 10½
Nags Head, North Carolina
Norm Taitz, Owner (252) 480-2000

This warm, friendly eatery has been a big hit with locals since it opened in 1992. Mulligan's serves traditional seafood, steaks and chicken with specials nightly and sushi served on Sunday. The restaurant occupies the former 1945 building that was known as Millers Drug Store before it was rennovated.

Lunch specials change daily. Soups and salads and a large variety of burgers and sandwiches are available from their lunch menu. The crabcake sandwich, chock full of crabmeat, is one of my favorites. Dinner entrees include shrimp scampi sautéed in garlic herb butter with capers and served over linguine; Coconut chicken, rolled in a coconut butter, fried and served with their own secret tropical sauce. Seasonal, regional seafood is the menu's main focus.

There is a full bar serving appetizers and light dinners or try oysters on the half shell or steamed from the raw bar. Live entertainment Wednesday through Sunday in season. Mulligan's is open year round for lunch and dinner.

## *Blackened Crawfish Cakes*

*Blackened Crawfish Cakes:*

2 oz. butter or margarine
⅛ c. minced garlic
1 lb. minced crawfish tails
2 medium green peppers, diced
3 ribs celery, diced
1 bunch green onions, diced
1 medium red pepper, diced
Juice from one lemon

*Spices:*

¼ tsp. ground white pepper
¼ tsp. cayenne pepper
¼ tsp. black pepper
¼ tsp. oregano
¼ tsp. basil
¼ tsp. thyme
¼ tsp. onion salt
¼ tsp. garlic salt
Pinch sugar
Pinch salt

*Binder:*

1 large egg
½ c. mayonnaise
1 to 1½ c. bread crumbs
Dash Worcestershire sauce

Method:
Mix all spices and set aside. Melt butter over medium heat. Add all vegetables and ½ c. spice mixture. Cook until tender. Add crawfish, remaining spices and lemon juice. Cook until heated thoroughly. Remove from heat, drain excess liquid, then cool. Add to binder. Portion 8 (4 oz.) cakes. Lightly dust cakes with Cajun seasonings. Blacken in cast iron skillet, keep warm.

*Fresh Tomato Basil Butter:*

½ c. seafood stock or
bottled clam juice
¼ c. fresh tomatoes, peeled,
seeded and diced
1 T. fresh basil leaves,
julienne
2 oz. raw butter, cubed
1 oz. white wine, optional

Method:
Bring stock, wine and tomatoes to boil in sauce pan. Boil gently until reduced to just over bottom of pan. Remove from heat, add basil leaves and butter (one piece at a time) until all butter is incorporated into sauce. Nap heated plates with sauce, top with blackened cakes and enjoy!

# North China Restaurant

Outer Banks Mall, MP 14 Bypass
Nags Head, North Carolina
Richard & Michael Lam, Owners/Chefs
Nags Head location (252) 441-3454
Kitty Hawk location (252) 261-5511

*North China Restaurant is the locals' most favorite Chinese restaurant on the Outer Banks. Whether the base is chicken, beef, or seafood, the character and flavor is rich and succulent. North China Restaurant offers the top quality and the best value of authentic Hunan, Mandarin, and Szechuan cuisine with the fine dining atmosphere. Banquet and party room is also available. Open year round.*

## Hunan Triple Crown

*Ingredients 1:*

6 oz. flank steak
12 pcs. 20-30 count scallops
8 pcs. jumbo shrimp
½ pc. square cut onion
Whole square-cut bell green pepper
½ sliced carrot
8 pcs. button mushroom
(cut ea. pc. in half)
Bamboo shoots (sliced)
Water chestnuts (sliced)
10 pcs. fresh snow peas

*Ingredients 2:*

⅓ rice vinegar
½ soupspoon chopped scallion
⅓ tsp. salt
1 tsp. sugar
½ soupspoon oyster sauce
(light sodium)
½ tsp. thick soy sauce
½ tsp. sesame oil
1 soupspoon rice wine
½ tsp. red chili pepper paste
½ tsp. chicken bouillon
1½ c. chicken broth

(Use a bowl to mix and stir all of the above ingredients.)

*Ingredients 3:*

3 slices ginger root
½ tsp. garlic (chopped)
½ tsp. black bean paste

Procedure:
Cut the flank steak into slices. Peel the shrimp under running water and cut three-fourths open up the back of the shrimp and take the vein out.

Marinate the beef, shrimp and scallops with egg white, cornstarch, and a little oil with water mixed.

Put about ½ soupspoon vegetable oil into a heated wok pan, then put the meat and seafoods in, stir-fry about ½ minute, then remove and drain out.

Put ½ soupspoon vegetable oil again into a heated wok pan, then put the ginger root, garlic and black bean paste (ingredients 3) into the heated oil and stir-fry good. Then put the meat, seafoods and all vegetables in and stir-fry about ½ minute. Add more heat to the wok to make it hotter, then pour in the 'ingredients 2' and continue stirring with the strong fire until the sauce becomes less sticky to the meats and vegetables; then put the snow peas and green peppers in and stir a little bit at the final stage. Serves 2 people.

# The Oasis Seafood Restaurant

7721 Virginia Dare Trail
Nags Head, North Carolina
Mike, Mark & Kellam France, Owners (252) 441-7721

*The Oasis Restaurant was founded in 1950 by Violet Kellam. The Oasis is noted for fresh local seafood, barefoot college co-eds and the home of lace cornbread.*

*The tradition has continued for 49 years, now operated by Ms. Kellam's grandsons Mike, Mark and Kellam France. The Oasis continues to be a mainstay for good food, casual atmosphere and friendly people. It is located on the Nags Head/Manteo causeway. The Oasis has a beautiful view of the Roanoke Sound, completed with majestic sunsets. Enjoy cocktails on the waterfront deck while listening to live music during summer months. The Oasis is a 115-seat waterfront restaurant.*

*Now patrons have the option to arrive by sea or land with the addition of the 250-foot dock space and a 500-square foot gazebo where patrons can sit and admire the view. The Oasis is still known as the "Landmark of the Outer Banks."*

## Tuna Oasis

7 oz. fresh tuna steak
½ c. sliced yellow onion
½ c. sliced green pepper
½ c. cubed pineapple w/juice
½ c. Major Greys Mango Chutney
Juice of ½ lemon
Dry white table wine
All-purpose flour with salt & pepper to taste
Virgin olive oil or margarine for sauté

Dredge fresh tuna steak in flour, salt and pepper mix. Place tuna in sauté pan with onions and peppers over medium-high heat using either margarine or olive oil.

Sauté for 2½ minutes, turn once and add lemon juice and white wine. Continue sautéing for additional 1½ minutes before reducing heat to low. Add Mango Chutney and pineapple juice, simmer for 2 minutes.

Remove tuna from pan and place on serving plate. Place onions and peppers on top and smother with sauce from pan. Garnish with chunk pineapple and parsley sprig. Serve with fresh steamed garden vegetable medley and rice pilaf. Our Favorite Dish!!! Enjoy!!!

# Ocean Boulevard

N.C. Hwy. 12 (Beach Road), MP 2
Kitty Hawk, North Carolina

Sam McGann & John Power, Owners (252) 261-2546
Thomas Power & Kris Mullins, Owners
Chuck Arnold, Executive Chef

This one-of-a-kind upscale award-winning restaurant is the result of Sam McGann's and John Power's nine successful years serving up quality cuisine at The Blue Point Bar & Grill in Duck. In September 1995 these two culinary masters opened Ocean Boulevard Bistro & Martini Bar and quickly became one of the most popular restaurants on the Outer Banks.

The restaurant occupies the former Virginia Dare Hardware Store and is now a haven for creative cocktails and sophisticated cuisine. The Martini Bar is made of simple concrete weighing four tons and other areas of dining area have exposed brick walls as well as retro glass block. The kitchen is exposed and even offers a "chefs counter" where guests can watch the culinary team in action.

The menu at Ocean Boulevard is the result of an evolving style refined over the years at The Blue Point by McGann with Chef Chuck Arnold. Selections are all prepared using locally grown herbs, spices, produce and fresh seafood. Menu changes according to the season.

Ocean Boulevard and The Blue Point Bar & Grill recently received a 3-star rating from the Mobile Guide, two of only three restaurants on the Outer Banks to receive this honor. In January 1998 Chef Thomas Power and Kris Mullins joined the company as partners.

Reservations are highly recommended. Open year round, for dinner only.

## *Grilled Pork Chop with Walnut & Gruyere Bread Pudding & Port Wine-Pear Sauce*

1 tsp. butter
2 c. french bread, diced
1½ c. Gruyere or Swiss cheese, grated
1 c. leeks, washed & diced
1 c. walnuts, crumbled
1 egg
1 c. cream
½ c. chicken stock
Salt as needed
Black pepper, cracked, to taste
6 8 oz. center cut pork chops
2 T. olive oil
1 c. Port Wine-Pear Sauce

*To prepare bread pudding*:
Preheat oven to 350 degrees. Grease a 9-inch baking pan with 1 tsp. butter.

In a large mixing bowl, toss bread, cheese, leeks and walnuts. Mix together. In a separate mixing bowl, combine eggs, cream and stock. Whisk together. Season with salt and pepper.

Press bread mixture into baking pan and cover evenly with egg and cream mixture. Bake bread pudding in a 350-degree oven for 30-35 minutes or until golden brown.

*To prepare pork chops*:
Prepare a gas or charcoal grill, or preheat a large cast iron pan. Brush pork chops with olive oil and season with salt and pepper, then grill on each side. Transfer to a baking pan and cook in the oven to 140 degrees internal temperature until about medium doneness. Serves 6.

## *Port Wine-Pear Sauce*

1¾ pear, peeled, cored, quartered
1 c. Port
1 c. red wine
½ c. sugar
2 T. butter
Juice of ¼ lemon

Bring pear, port, sugar and wine to simmer in medium saucepan. Cook for 30 minutes until liquid is reduced by one-fourth, approximately ½ cup. Place sauce in a food processor and purée. Return to stove and add butter, whisking continuously over low heat. Add lemon juice.

To plate:
Warm six dinner plates. Cut bread pudding into six wedges. Place a wedge on each plate. Lean a pork chop on the bread pudding. Sauce each plate with 2 oz. Port Wine-Pear Sauce. Accompany the dish with a warm vegetable, such as sautéed spinach.

# *Orange Blossom Café and Bakery*

*N.C. Hwy. 12*
*Buxton, North Carolina*

*Henry & Michal Schliff, Owners* *(252) 995-4109*

*The Orange Blossom is a great place for islanders to come together and for tourists to gather, located in the heart of "downtown" Buxton, and in eye sight of the Cape Hatteras Lighthouse. It's a great place to start your day with an array of fresh baked sweets and just baked donuts, fluffy biscuits and fresh bagels, and, of course, those famous Apple Uglies that you have to see to believe.*

*Now into its eighth year, this wonderful café serves great Mexican cuisine, salads and fresh bread sandwiches so high you'll wonder how it's possible to eat the whole thing.*

*Henry and Michal have a wonderful cookbook out, appropriately called "Meet Me at the Orange Blossom." They have included anecdotes and stories about the recipes and their years of living on Hatteras Island. The restaurant is open from 7 a.m. until 2 p.m. daily.*

## *Cranberry-Orange Blossom Muffins*

1½ sticks butter, softened
1⅓ c. sugar
4 large eggs
4 c. flour
4 tsp. baking powder
1 tsp. salt
2 tsp. grated orange rind
1⅓ c. milk
½ tsp. orange extract
2 c. fresh cranberries
⅔ c. chopped pecans

In an electric mixer, cream the butter and sugar. Beat in the eggs one at a time. Combine the flour, baking powder, salt and orange rind. Beat the flour mixture and milk alternately into the creamed mixture. Add the orange extract and fold into the cranberries and pecans. Scoop into 12 well greased muffin cups and bake in a 350-degree oven until an inserted toothpick comes out clean. Cool on a wire rack for a few minutes and remove muffins from pan. Spread tops with orange icing.

*Orange Icing*

1¾ c. powdered sugar
2 T. orange juice
2 T. orange marmalade

Heat the marmalade briefly to liquefy. Place sugar in the bowl of an electric mixer and beat in the orange juice and marmalade to obtain a spreading consistency.

# Owens Restaurant

Mile Post 16½, Beach Road
Nags Head, North Carolina
Owens Family, Owners (252) 441-7309
Clara Mae Shannon, Operator

*Is Owens Restaurant a great restaurant or an institution on the Outer Banks? Of course, the answer has to be, both. Owens Restaurant was established in 1946 by Bob and Clara Owens. Their goal was to serve only the freshest seafood and shellfish at a reasonable price, and make the customer feel like family. Owens is still run that way after 50 years. Over the years the family has collected many nautical artifacts that are displayed in the restaurant. No visit to the Outer Banks would be complete without a visit to this historic restaurant. Bob and Clara would be proud to know that their children, grandchildren, and great-grandchildren are still carrying on their proud tradition.*

*Owens now focuses more on classic Southern coastal cuisine, such as shrimp and grits, or pecan-encrusted Carolina catfish. Miss O' crabcakes and pastas are among the most popular entrees. The menu features fresh Maine lobster, aged Angus beef, ribs, pasta, fresh produce and herbs. The homemade desserts are definitely worth saving room for.*

## Owens' Hush Puppies

2½ c. self-rising flour
1 c. white cornmeal
⅔ c. sugar
1 T. baking powder
1 tsp. salt
1 egg
1¼ c. cold water
¼ c. evaporated milk

Mix first 5 ingredients thoroughly; add egg and blend in well. Combine milk with cold water; pour all liquid into the dry mixture. Mix gently but quickly, just enough to blend everything together. Allow to rest 10 minutes at room temperature; drop by rounded teaspoonfuls into 325-degree vegetable oil. Fry, rolling frequently, until golden brown; 6 to 8 minutes. Dip spoon in cold water after dropping each spoonful.

# The Pelican Restaurant

Hwy. 12, P.O. Box 447
Ocracoke Island, North Carolina
Lisa Caricofe & Sydney Mulder, Owners (252) 928-7431
Sherry Atkinson & Jason Wells, Chefs

*The Pelican Restaurant is located in the heart of Ocracoke Village. The main house was built in the 1800s with additions being added later, still keeping the traditional Ocracoke housing feel. The screened-in front porch offers relief from the heat during the summer or a cozy fireside meal in the winter.*

*In addition to this is the Tiki Bar—a favorite local hangout; featuring daily specials and cool beverages to help you ease into our island ways.*

*The Pelican offers a fresh succulent array of local seafood and other entrees. Be it breakfast, lunch or dinner, they are sure that they can appease your appetite.*

## Crabcakes

3 eggs
¼ c. milk
5 dashes Worcestershire sauce
¼ c. mayonnaise
¾ c. Dijon mustard
2 shallots, chopped fine
1 bunch of scallions
2 T. flour
1 dash Tabasco
¼ c. parsley
1 tsp. garlic powder
2 tsp. Old Bay seasoning
½ tsp. white pepper
7 slices white bread, crust removed (cut into squares)
2 lb. *picked* crab meat

Blend ingredients well before adding bread. Add bread pieces and mix well with both hands. Toss *lightly* with hands.

These crabcakes may be placed onto a flat grill or a fry pan. Use very little butter or coating. *Do not fry*--they will break apart. Once the first side towards the heat sets up (approximately 3 minutes), flip and cook until done.

# Penguin Isle

Soundside Grill & Bar
US Hwy. 158 Bypass, MP 16
Nags Head, North Carolina

Doug Tutwiler &, Mike Kelly, owners (252) 441-2637
Lee Miller, Executive Chef

*Located on the beautiful Roanoke Sound, this elegant restaurant has been awarded 3 Diamonds by AAA and has won The Wine Spectator's Award of Excellence for its wine list as "one of the best in the world" for the past six years.*

*The decor here is tasteful and creative, with paintings and pictures of coastal life, ship models, and carved decoys. Tables are set with crystal glassware on fine white linen tablecloths.*

*Penguin Isle's food is as seductive as its surroundings. Fresh local seafood, chicken, duck, handmade pasta, Black Angus beef, and fresh baked breads are only a part of their offerings. All the desserts are delectable.*

*A separate lounge with a full bar overlooks the sound where spectacular sunsets can be enjoyed while having a cocktail before dinner.*

## Shrimp Aristotle

1½ lbs. shrimp, peel and devein, medium size (26-30)
2 large tomatoes, diced
1 green bell pepper, julienne
8 mushrooms, sliced
2 T. fresh garlic, minced
1 zucchini squash, medium size, washed and julienne
2 tsp. olive oil
Salt & pepper, to taste
4 oz. feta cheese crumbled and drained
1 c. heavy cream
1 T. water
½ lb. fresh Scallion Fettuccine or fresh store-bought pasta
2 T. butter

Peel shrimp, slice vegetables. Simmer heavy cream till reduced to ⅔ cup or slightly thickened; do not let cream boil over side of pot. Season with a little salt and pepper. Place reduced cream off to side, off heat. Heat olive oil in large sauté pan, add shrimp, garlic, salt and pepper; cook for 30 seconds. Add all vegetables, water and season with salt and pepper. Cook till shrimp are pink and vegetables are hot. Cook homemade fettucine or store-bought till al dente (30-45 seconds). Toss drained fettuccine with butter, reduce cream and feta cheese. Top pasta with vegetables and shrimp and serve on warm plates. Serve immediately. Serves 4.

## Peppercorn's Restaurant & Lounge

Ramada Inn
1701 Virginia Dare Trail MP 9.5
Kill Devil Hills, North Carolina
Sterling Webster, General Manager (252) 441-2151 ext. 665
Mark Pennington, Erik Speer, Chefs

Ocean views are spectacular at this great restaurant overlooking the Atlantic. You can dine and watch the pelicans glide over the waves or the moon rise over the ocean while enjoying a delightful dinner. Their classically trained chefs bring a combination of Multi-ethnic foods and Mediterranean dishes as well as a very creative cosmopolitan flair to the menu.

Local favorites include Italian Risotto with shrimp, scallops and crabmeat made with the freshest seafood, rice and mixed cheese; Atlantic salmon stuffed with crabmeat, and prime rib crusted with spices and served au jus. Crabcakes are also a favorite, seasoned with just the right amount of spices. Each entrée is served with herb roasted potatoes or rice pilaf and fresh vegetables and a basket of breads. You'll definitely want to try some of the wonderful desserts prepared by Erik. For lunch, you'll want to try the giant Portabello mushroom stuffed with spiced crabmeat and melted cheese or the soups, salads, and sandwiches.

An outside Gazebo deck bar offers lunch with live acoustic music from 1-6 p.m. daily in season. There's a full bar with live entertainment nightly during the summer. A children's menu is available. Open for breakfast, lunch, and dinner year round.

## *Portobello Mushroom Stuffed With Crabmeat*

2 tablespoon Olive oil
1 teaspoon crushed garlic
4 ounces fresh lump crabmeat
2 ounces shredded Cheddar, Swiss or Parmesan cheese
Juice of 1 lemon
Dash of Old Bay seasoning, salt and pepper

**Method:**

1. Preheat oven to broil.
2. 1 large Portobello mushroom cap, stem removed
   Marinate mushroom cap in olive oil and crushed garlic for 15 min.
3. Top mushroom with remaining ingredients, sprinkling the shredded cheese on top.
4. Place on a lightly oiled baking pan.
5. Put under preheated broiler until heated through and cheese is melted and light brown. Approximately 5 to 7 minutes.
6. Serve whole with a salad and dressing of choice or cut into wedges and serve as an appetizer.

Serves 1 as Entrée or 2 as an Appetizer

# Pony Island Restaurant

N.C. Hwy. 12
Ocracoke, North Carolina

Sue O'Neal, Owner (252) 928-5701

*Since 1960 this casual, down home restaurant has served up some of the best and freshest seafood around, which keeps people coming back time after time. Big breakfasts of biscuits, hotcakes, omelettes and the famous Pony Potatoes--hash browns with melted cheese, salsa, and sour cream--make this restaurant an all-time favorite place for breakfast.*

*Seafood platters come with a combination of fish, scallops, oysters, shrimp, clam strips, and crabcake. If you wish, you can even bring your own fish (provided you cleaned it), and they'll cook it for you. Chicken, beef and southwestern dishes are also served. You won't want to miss trying the Seafood Gumbo Soup, it's a favorite. Don't forget to try some of their freshly baked homemade desserts.*

## Seafood Gumbo

Shrimp/Scallops (diced)
Lemon juice
Margarine-butter combination
Onion
Leek
Celery
Flour
Canned tomatoes
Bay leaf
Creole seasoning
Fresh ground black pepper
Okra
Rice

## *Port O' Call Restaurant and Saloon*

*Virginia Dare Road (Beach Road), MP 8½*
*Kill Devil Hills, North Carolina*
*Frank H. Gajar, Owner* (252) 441-7484

*The Port O' Call was founded in 1965 and has been in continuous operation ever since. In 1983, a major renovation and expansion was undertaken to add a gift shop and lounge.*

*Our lounge features live entertainment every night, in season, and the gift shop is open year round. The interior design of the Port O' Call is turn of the century Victorian with period furniture and collectibles throughout.*

*The menu features a large selection of seafood, steaks, pasta, veal and chicken, including a children's menu. A Brunch buffet is served every Sunday.*

### *Caribbean Jerk Wahoo*

2 lbs. Wahoo fillets
1 T. Caribbean Jerk Seasoning
¼ c. white wine
¼ c. orange juice
1 tsp. white pepper
¼ c. fresh cilantro

Combine seasoning, pepper, cilantro, and liquids. Pour over fillets and bake in 350-degree oven for 10 minutes.

Meanwhile, heat together the following:
1 8 oz. can coconut milk
1 tsp. brown sugar
1 tsp. crab base

Heat until sugar and crab base are dissolved.

To this mixture add:
¼ c. chopped green onion
¼ c. each, diced yellow, green and sweet red peppers
½ c. fresh pineapple chunks

Cook over medium to low heat for 15 minutes. Add ⅛ tsp. crushed red pepper and ¼ c. lemon juice. Heat for 2-3 minutes. Add salt to taste. Pour over fillets and garnish with toasted coconut.

# Pots On -N- Kitchen

Hwy. 158
Harbinger, North Carolina
(252) 491-2544

*On the way to the Outer Banks, a traveler passes through many small towns on the Currituck peninsula. In the summers of 1985 and 1986 in Harbinger, Joyce Hines and Ginger Bowden ran a roadside vegetable market. To make better use of their fresh produce, the two Currituck natives decided to open a restaurant, and the Pots On -N- Kitchen was born. After five years, ownership of the restaurant passed to Ginger Bowden's nieces and has been owned by the same families since. A favorite of locals and a pleasant surprise for seasonal visitors, Pots On -N- Kitchen specializes in country cooking in a relaxed family environment.*

*Serving breakfast, lunch and dinner all year, Pots On -N- Kitchen has established its reputation with menu items that are sure to please anyone. Lunch and dinner specials change daily, and are as diverse as Meatloaf, Prime Rib and Crab Imperial. All specials, desserts and vegetable dishes are homemade and prepared fresh daily. Vegetable dishes also change seasonally to ensure freshness and quality. One of the Pots On -N- Kitchen's staple desserts, featured at every lunch and dinner meal, is Hershey Pie. Simple, yet delicious, it's a perfect way to finish a meal at Pots On -N- Kitchen.*

## Hershey Pie

5 Hershey Bars
16 oz. cool whip
2 T. butter
1 graham cracker pie shell

Melt chocolate bars and butter until smooth. Stir in 8 oz. cool whip. Fold into pie shell. Top with remaining cool whip. Decorate with chocolate sprinkles.

# *Quagmires*

*1315 N. Virginia Dare Trail, MP 7½*
*Kill Devil Hills, North Carolina*
*John Kirchmier, Owner* *(252) 441-9188*
*Judy Fisher & Charles Kirchmier, Owners*
*Bunky Calvert, Head Chef*

*The original frame and cedar shake building with its dormer windows is all that remains of the original 1925 Croatan Lodge, now known as Quagmires. In 1996 John Kirchmier purchased the property because he could not stand the thought of it being torn down.*

*Despite the changes, Quagmires still specializes in fresh local seafood, pastas, beef, chicken and some Mexican favorites. One of my favorite dishes is the Chicken and Crab Enchilada combination.*

*Located upstairs is a large bar with an incredible view of the ocean and two large decks that stay packed during the summer months. Casual and fun, Quags is a cool place for big and little kids. Quagmires is open seven days a week for lunch and dinner in season.*

## *Shrimp Diablo*

½ oz. olive oil
1 oz. diced onion
2 oz. diced tomato
½ oz. sliced jalapeno
8 each large fresh shrimp
½ c. heavy cream
½ oz. Cajun seasoning
Salt to taste
Pepper to taste
1 c. cooked rice
½ oz. Texas Pete wing sauce

In sauté pan over medium heat, add first 5 ingredients. Cook until shrimp are opaque, add Cajun seasoning, salt and pepper. Add heavy cream and wing sauce. Sauté until cream reduces one-third.

Serve over plate of rice, arrange shrimp around border of plate, garnish with lemon wheel and scallion flower. Serves 1. (You may make it for any number, just increase the amounts.)

# *Queen Anne's Revenge Restaurant*

*P.O. Box 427*
*Wanchese, North Carolina*
*Wayne & Nancy Gray, Owners* (252) 473-5466
*Wayne Gray, Chef*

*Queen Anne's Revenge Restaurant, founded in 1978, is located in Wanchese on the southern end of Roanoke Island. Despite its remote location, Queen Anne's Revenge has built up a loyal following of long-time customers. Chef Wayne Gray, who also owns the restaurant along with his wife, Nancy, is uncompromising in his selection of fine seafood and steak.*

*The restaurant was named for one of Blackbeard's pirate ships. Recently the famous sunken vessel was discovered a few miles offshore from Beaufort, North Carolina.*

## *Posh Squash*

2 lbs. zucchini or yellow squash, sliced
2 eggs
1 small onion, chopped
¼ green pepper, diced
1 c. mayonnaise
1 c. Parmesan cheese
Black pepper
Italian bread crumbs

Cook squash until tender. Let drain at least ½ hour. Mix together eggs, onion, green pepper, mayonnaise, cheese and black pepper. Fold in squash. Top with bread crumbs and bake at 350 degrees for 25 minutes.

# Rick and Tina Saul's Cafe

P.O. Box 35, Highway 158
Harbinger, North Carolina
Rick & Tina Saul, Owners (252) 491-5000

*This is a down home country cafe with good food at a good price. Bring the whole family in, sit down and dine, all-you-can-eat family style. They bring the food to your table and gladly fill each bowl as it is emptied.*

*Although they serve other things, this cafe is best represented by their delicious barbecue. The name "Saul" is synonymous with East Carolina style barbecue. Rick Saul, although young in years, is no newcomer to the restaurant business. He literally grew up in his father's restaurant.*

*Stop by. If you are lucky, you may get a glimpse of the newest little Saul keeping mom company.*

## Chocolate Ribbon Pie

4 oz. Philadelphia cream cheese, softened
2 T. sugar
1 T. milk
1 8 oz. tub Cool Whip topping
1 prepared 9-in. chocolate-flavored crumbs pie crust
2 c. cold milk
2 packages (4-serving size) Jello chocolate pudding/pie filling
Dark milk chocolate, refrigerated

Combine the softened cream cheese, sugar and 1 T. milk in a large bowl and beat on low speed until smooth. Gently fold in one half of the whipped topping and spread this mixture over the bottom of pie crust. Combine 2 c. milk and the pudding mix into a large bowl and whisk until the mixture thickens; about 2 minutes. Pour the pudding mixture over the cream cheese mixture, and refrigerate the pie for 4 hours or until set. Just before you serve the pie, top it with the other half of whipped topping. Garnish with shaved dark chocolate.

# The Roadside Bar and Grill

1193 Duck Road
Duck, North Carolina
Mark & Ashley Copeland, Owners (252) 261-5729
Matt Frettwell, Executive Chef

The Roadside Bar and Grill is located in an antique cottage in the heart of Duck Village. The structure was originally built in 1932 by Mr. and Mrs. J. E. Hines as their residence. It was one of the first homes in Duck. The building has also been used a real estate office and a retail shop. The renovations which created the restaurant began in November of 1994. The floors were stripped down to their original hard wood, an open air kitchen was created, and a large brick patio was added. The doors opened for business in May of 1995.

The following recipe is a good representation of the menu at The Roadside. Chef Matt Frettwell uses only the freshest ingredients. He buys the fish from local fishermen and the produce from a Wanchese farm, then adds a great deal of imagination and creativity during the preparation. We hope you will enjoy this recipe and pay us a visit next time you are in Duck.

## *Bronzed Tuna*

with Portabello-Ardsville Sesame Orzo & Mango Salsa

*Bronzed Tuna*:

10 oz. tuna steak
1 tsp. cayenne
1 tsp. red pepper
1 tsp. crushed red pepper
1 tsp. black pepper
1 tsp. salt
1 tsp. oregano
1 tsp. rosemary
1 tsp. thyme
3½ T. sugar
¾ c. oil

*Orzo*:

2 c. cooked orzo
3 T. diced Andsville sausage
3 T. diced roasted portabello
4 T. sesame oil
1 T. kosher salt
1 tsp. white pepper
1 T. Caribbean jerk

*Mango Salsa*:

1 c. mango diced
3 T. diced red onion
3 T. diced red pepper
3 T. diced scallions
2 squeezed limes
1 tsp. cayenne
2 oz. Malibu rum

Bronze Mix: Add all ingredients together until they form a smooth paste.
Orzo: Mix cooked orzo and ingredients and saute lightly.
Salsa: Add all ingredients and refrigerate.

Cooking and Serving: In well ventilated area, heat skillet on high heat. Dredge tuna in bronze mix until well coated. Sear on both sides of tuna and place on top of sauteed orzo mix, then top with mango salsa.

# Rundown Café

N.C. Hwy. 12, Beach Road MP 1
Kitty Hawk, North Carolina

Will Thorp, Owner (252) 255-0026

*Caribbean flavors join local seafood to create the theme of this locals favorite dining spot. Opened in 1993, this popular restaurant was an expansion of the tropics for the northern beaches and quickly became a vacationers favorite. The Caribbean-themed menu and the tropical island décor has kept year round residents returning to this spot.*

*Named for a Jamaican stew, Rundown serves favorites such as stuffed chicken with sautéed spinach and feta cheese oven roasted and toped with a roasted red pepper sauce. Other favorites include the Rundown Noodles, Caribbean style vegetarian rice noodles with sautéed veggies in a spicy Thai sauce topped with ground peanuts and lime. Specials are listed daily on a large board and change nightly. The desserts are definitely worth trying, especially the dark chocolate brownie, and the chocolate mint cheese cake.*

*There's a full bar where you can kick back and be with the gang. Live music and an oceanview deck make this a jewel of a find. Rundown Café is a place you'll feel comfortable, no matter what your age or lifestyle. There's a cultural, social-economic barrier-less crowd that you find here. The restaurant is closed in December. Open for lunch and dinner daily in season.*

## St. Martin Shrimp

48 peeled and deveined shrimp (31-35) ct.
1 yellow onion julienned
2 bulbs garlic, chopped
3 tomatoes, diced
¼ cup sundried tomatoes julienned
8 pieces of bacon, cooked and chopped
¼ cup olive oil
½ stick butter
chopped parsley
salt and pepper
½ cup white wine
1 small box of linguini, cooked

Get olive oil hot in large skillet. Sauté garlic & onion. Cook til garlic starts to brown, add bacon and shrimp, sauté on high til starting to turn pink, add fresh tomatoes and sundried tomatoes, toss, Add white wine and let cook 2 minutes. Add salt, pepper to taste, let reduce, then toss in whole butter and chopped parsley. Drop pasta in hot salted water, Separate in 4 bowls. Top with shrimp mixture. Serve with parmesan cheese, and a piece of crusty French bread. Enjoy!!! Serves 4 P.S. You can't add enough garlic!

# RV's

Nags Head/Manteo Causeway
Nags Head, North Carolina

R.V. Owens, Owner (252) 441-4963

*R V's has been a favorite dining restaurant spot of visitors and locals alike since 1981. Located on the beautiful Roanoke Sound and Sugar Creek, dining here is to enjoy the best views and sunsets that the Outer Banks has to offer.*

*There's no better place to enjoy true Carolina seafood in a casual and laid back atmosphere other than RV's. They are known for their generous portions, great prices and treating guest as family. The Seafood Stew (recipe below) is a favorite amongst guest. Appetizers, steamed seafood, drink specials are served at the gazebo raw bar from June—Labor Day. There's also a full service bar inside.*

*A new gift shop has been added this year. RV's is open from mid February through November serving lunch and dinner seven days a week.*

## RV's Seafood Stew

1 slice bacon, chopped
3 stalks celery, coarsely chopped
1 carrot, peeled and shredded
½ onion, diced

1 tsp. salt
½ tsp. pepper
1 tsp. Old Bay seasoning
½ tsp. lemon pepper seasoning

Simmer above ingredients, stirring frequently until celery is about three-fourths cooked. Add ½ gal. Shrimp stock—either made from shrimp base or boiled shrimp shells. Add 3 lb. fresh diced tomatoes (3 lb. can of salsa style diced tomatoes may be substituted). Bring to boil. Add 2 lbs. raw (70/90 count), peeled and deveined shrimp along with 1 lb. scallops. Sea scallops are preferred but Bay scallops may be substituted. Return to a boil to be sure seafood is completely cooked. Reduce heat to low. Add 1-1/2 lb. of raw, diced potatoes, (diced baby red potatoes may be substituted). Cover and allow potatoes to cook on low heat for about ½ hour, stirring occasionally.
Makes approximately 1 ½ -2 gallons

# Sanderling Inn Restaurant

1461 Duck Road, N.C. Hwy. 12
Duck, North Carolina

Glen Aurand, C.E.C. Executive Chef (252) 449-6654
Mark Harrison, Chef d'Parte'

The first structure on this stretch of sand was built in 1874 but was replaced in 1899 with the Caffey's Inlet U.S. Lifesaving Station and was manned by brave souls to save shipwrecked seafarers. Today, that station houses the Sanderling Restaurant, a part of the famous Sanderling Inn Resort. The restaurant's dining room, a mixture of polished wood furnishings and nautical mementos, was once the station's boathouse. Throughout the restaurant are reminders of another era in time, an enormous bell for fog warnings, a Lyle gun, even a large ship's compass and a ship's wheel in the Swan Bar.

The Sanderling Restaurant is one of the Outer Banks' most acclaimed restaurants serving Southern Regional Cuisine for breakfast, lunch and dinner. The menu of imaginatively prepared dishes, including fresh seafood specialties, local grown vegetables, certified Angus beef, is complemented by an extensive selection of domestic and imported wines. The three-course Sunday brunch is the best on the beach. The lunch menu features soups, salads, sandwiches, and other daily specials.

Dinner entrees include Roasted Rainbow Trout stuffed with Brie, sweet peppers and lump crabmeat, with cream corn sauce over wild rice. A child's menu is available and reservations are strongly encouraged during prime season. The restaurant is opened year-round.

## *Shrimp, Corn, and Crab Chowder*

4 slices bacon
6 cups chicken stock or broth
½ lemon, pits removed
2 lbs. fresh shrimp
2 T. butter
1 medium onion, minced
2 celery ribs, minced
2 T. minced green bell pepper
2 cups frozen corn, thawed

Salt, freshly ground pepper
Tabasco
1 cup heavy cream
2 small carrots,
( sliced paper thin)
½ red bell pepper,
(cut into very small cubes)
3 oz. Sautéed Lump Crab

Fry the bacon till crisp, drain on paper towels, pour off all but 2 tablespoons of grease and crumble the bacon. In a large saucepan, combine one-half the chicken stock, the lemon half (squeezed), and the shrimp. Bring to a boil, remove from heat, cover and let stand 3 minutes. Drain the shrimp in a colander, pouring the hot stock into another large, heavy saucepan. Discard the lemon half. When cool enough to handle, shell and devein the shrimp. Reserve 12 shrimp, put remainder of the shrimp though a blender or food processor with the remaining stock.

In a skillet, heat the reserved bacon grease and butter, add the onion, celery and green pepper, and saute over low heat about 3 minutes or till vegetables are soft. Add the corn to the shrimp mixture and cook over moderate heat for 2 minutes, stirring. Add the sauteed vegetables to the mixture, stir, bring to a brisk boil, reduce heat and cook 2 minutes.

Remove from the heat, add seasonings to taste, cover and let stand 30 minutes. When ready to serve, bring chowder almost to a boil, stir in heavy cream, carrots, and red pepper cubes, and taste for seasoning. Ladle the chowder into heated soup plates and garnish each portion with crabmeat plus a sprinkling of crumbled bacon. Serves 6

# *Slammin Sammy's*

*Offshore Grille & Stillery*
*U.S. Hwy 158, MP 10½*
*Nags Head, North Carolina*

*Sammy Moore, Owner* *(252) 449-2255*
*Charlie Griffin, Chef*

*Slammin Sammy's is the premier sports bar on the Outer Banks featuring 27 TVs including 3 giant screens, shuffleboard and pool tables. It's the hot spot to meet new friends or just have dinner with old friends.*

*Lunch and dinner is served here with the dining area separate from the large sports bar. The dining area has recently been expanded to include an additional 40 seats. Sammy's offers a wide variety of menu items to choose from. There is no shortage of appetizers on this menu. Soups, chowders, salads, Po Boys, down east steamers, sandwiches of all kinds, pizza and seafood are served for lunch and dinner. All entrees include your choice of baked red potatoes or french fries, vegetable of the day or salad.*

*Sammy's was the winner of the 1998 Chili Peppers Cook-Off for their homemade from scratch meat chili. It is served in a bread bowl with melted cheddar cheese. It is definitely a winner. Slammin Sammy's is open year round.*

## *Slammin Sammy's Carolina Crabcakes*

2 lbs. lump crabmeat
¼ c. bread crumbs
1 T. Worchestershire sauce
2 T. parsley flakes
1 tsp. Old Bay seasoning
1 tsp. mustard
2 T. mayonnaise
2 eggs

Combine and mix all <u>but</u> crabmeat (add last). Mix crabmeat into mixture very gently. Make cakes and coat with fine seasoned bread crumbs. Fry or broil and enjoy!

# Sorrel Pacific Cuisine

Timbuck II Shopping Center, Soundside
Corolla, North Carolina

Martha and Earl Rice, Owners (252) 453-6979
Jennefer and G.James Spence, Owners
G. James Spence, Executive Chef

This lively restaurant is known for its delicious and unique dishes with a Far East taste and the only eatery in Corolla with a water view. Pacific Cuisine is food that is flavored with Japanese, Chinese, Vietnamese, Thai or Hawaiian spices to give it that extra twist.

For lunch, try Wasabi seared tuna or the stir-fry vegetable bowl with either chicken or shrimp. A mango burger served with mango chutney or a tiki tavern burger with bacon, hearts of palm and cheese, Portabella mushroom sandwich and shrimp melts are also favorites. Dinners at Sorrel include signature entrees such as crisp roast duckling drizzled in a chinese orange plum sauce with sautéed vegetables and whipped potatoes, grilled salmon with a cantonese black bean sauce, crab cakes illuminated by South Pacific mango, and sweet pepper chutney. You will want to try the Asian vegetable spring rolls or the corn, crab and pepper fritters that are listed on the creative appetizer list.

Enjoy a Margarita, Mai Tai, or a tropical smoothie in the new Teki Bar overlooking the water or sit outside on the patio and savor a drink or meal. Wednesday night's in the Teki bar features *live entertainment until 2 a.m. Wine and beer are available. The steamed seafood bar offers crab legs, shrimp, and other featured seafood specials. Sushi and Sashimi are served nightly*

*Now in its fifth season, Sorrel will be extending its Sunday Brunch hours in the summer. Brunch will include favorites such as Japanese omelettes, appetizers, pork short ribs, tropical fruit salads and corn, crab & pepper fritters. A children's menu is offered. The restaurant is open year round serving lunch and dinner. Reservations are recommended.*

## *Soba Noodle Salad*

- ¾ tsp. soy sauce
- ¾ tsp. Sesame Oil
- 4 oz. Japanese Soba Noodles, Cooked
- 2 T. red peppers, diced
- 2 T. yellow peppers, diced
- 2 T. snow peas, sliced
- 2 T. water chestnuts, sliced
- 2 T. carrots, julienned
- 2 ¼ tsp. Cilantro, chopped
- ¼ tsp. Sesame seeds, toasted

Mix together Soy sauce, Sesame oil, salt and pepper to taste. Add noodles and vegetables, 2 tablespoons of Cilantro, toss to coat. Place on bed of lettuce, sprinkle with Sesame seeds. Serves 1

# Swan Cove Restaurant

1174 Duck Road
Duck, North Carolina
Larry Herron & Richard Herron, Owners (252) 255-0500
Don Jester, Head Chef

Perched high on a dune with unbelievable views of the Currituck Sound, Swan Cove has established itself as one of the finer establishments in the Duck area. The soundfront dining room offers views from every angle. Tablecloths and cut flowers adorn each table in this light and airy restaurant.

Only the freshest seafood, local vegetables and fresh herbs are used in preparation. Entrees include pork chops, fresh local seafood, duck, pastas, steaks, and fresh salads. For starters, try the Lobster Ravioli stuffed with fresh lobster in a pool of cognac tomato cream. The menu changes frequently.

Swan Cove is only open in season serving lunch and dinner. A children's menu is available. Call for reservations.

## Exotic Prawns Kabobs

1 lb. Prawns
1/3 cup Soy sauce
1/3 cup olive oil
1/3 cup sherry
½ tsp. onion powder
½ tsp. garlic powder
½ tsp. ginger
½ tsp. pepper

Peel and devein prawns, skewer with bamboo. Place in shallow pan. Blend ingredients together and pour over prawns. Marinate for 30 minutes. Grill for 3 minutes on each side or until prawn turn pink.

# *Top Dog Café*

*Highway 12*
*Waves, North Carolina*

*Joe & Pat Wolfe, Owners* (252) 987-1272

*Top Dog Café was established in Waves in 1995 by Joe and Pat Wolfe, two "corporate refugees" who naively wanted to open up a "simple hot dog place" on Hatteras Island in order to escape the "big city rat race". The café has since had to expand to survive, focuses more on burgers than dogs, and the Wolfes have aged considerably as the "rat race" now comes to them looking for good food while they are on vacation.*

*The café expanded to include a relaxing, screened-in porch with a rustic nautical theme to reflect the personality of the island. The menu features huge, old-fashioned burgers (among other things) with an assortment of specialty toppings to tempt even the most discriminating taste buds. The burgers range in size from a ½-lb. "Big Kahoona" to a whopping 1-lb. "'Sunami." Those with huge appetites and a sense of adventure try the triple-decker "'Sunami" version of the "Wild Thing" burger!*

## *"Wild Thing" Burger*

½ lb. low-fat ground beef
⅓ c. chopped onions
1 T. vegetable oil
¼ c. sliced jalapenos
½ c. grated Monterey Jack cheese

Sauté chopped onions in vegetable oil till softened. Cover, drain and place onions in a bowl to the side. Form ground beef into a patty and fry in pan over medium heat until browned on one side, then turn over and brown on other side till well done but still juicy. Cover pan and drain. Sprinkle grated Monterey Jack cheese over burger, cover pan and heat until cheese melts. Remove cover and top burger with sautéed onions and jalapenos. Serve on 5-inch seeded bun with lettuce and tomato, if desired. If a spicier "hot" taste is desired, jalapenos should be heated in pan for 1 minute before placing on burger to release additional "heat." Beware! Do not hover over pan as jalapenos are heated unless you want to clear your sinuses and burn your throat and eyes. The fumes are wild!

# Tortugas' Lie Restaurant

P.O. Box 1963, MP 11
Nags Head, North Carolina
Bob Sanders, Owner-Manager (252) 441-7299
Richard Welch, Owner-Chef

*Tortugas' Lie Restaurant has a growing reputation as being one of the area's best moderately priced restaurants that continues to serve the most appetizing food on the Outer Banks. The menu features Caribbean-inspired seafood, chicken, beef and vegetarian dishes for lunch and dinner. Tortugas' also offers a full raw and steamed bar, as well as speciality drinks, wine, buckets of beer and micro beers in the bottle or on tap. The chef's knowledge of spicy jerk seasoning and fruit-based sauces turns ordinary beef, chicken and seafood dishes into a culinary delight.*

*Tortugas' has a very casual come-as-you-are type atmosphere which lends to its menu; there are even two beach volleyball courts right out back. You may order something as simple as a grilled fish burrito or hamburger right off the beach, or come in to dine on an entree of grilled marinated mahi-mahi topped with a spicy pineapple salsa. So stop by and give them a try, and don't forget to take your volleyball.*

## Saint Martin Shrimp

1 lb. shrimp, peeled & deveined
2 c. coarse chopped tomatoes
1 lb. cooked fettuccine
1 small to medium red onion, julienne
4 T. minced fresh garlic
4 T. bacon, cooked & chopped
(op. for veggies)
½ c. Parmesan cheese, freshly grated
¼ c. chopped fresh parsley
½ c. dry white wine
Salt & pepper to taste
¼ c. olive oil
¼ c. butter

Sauté garlic and red onion in the olive oil until soft over medium to high heat. Add shrimp, stir, cook 1 minute, and add tomatoes, bacon, parsley, salt and pepper. Cook 1 minute and continue to stir. Deglaze pan with white wine and reduce liquid by one-half by cooking down with medium heat. Stir in pasta and butter over medium heat and cook until pasta is hot. Serve hot with fresh grated Parmesan cheese. Serves 4.

# Weeping Radish Brewery & Bavarian Restaurant

U.S. Hwy. 64
Manteo, North Carolina
Uli Bennewitz, Owner (252) 473-1157
Stephan Murst, Executive Chef

As soon as you pass the Christmas Shop, you will notice a large Bavarian restaurant known as The Weeping Radish. This is definitely an eatery that should be tried for German food and beer. Bavarian décor prevails throughout this two-story dining room where waitress greet you in Bavarian dress.

Traditional German meals include Sauerbraten, Wiener Schnitzel, roasted pork loin (Schweinebraten), and the Weeping Radish Sampler. For a real taste of Bavaria-try their Bauernwurst, Bratwurst, Knackfrisch or a combination platter. American favorites served include stuffed chicken breast, prime rib, salads. Sandwiches, salads, soups, and other German specialties are served for lunch.

A full bar separate from the restaurant is a great place to meet. This restaurant has an outdoor beer garden serving their own microbrewery beer. The Weeping Radish microbrewery opened in 1986 offering pure, fresh German beer without chemical additives and preservatives. Beer can be purchased to take home. Uli Bennewitz gives week-day talks and sampling of his beer. It's well worth the time to check this out.

Open for lunch and dinner year round.

## Weeping Radish Bavarian Lambchops

8 lambchops
Chopped celery, onion, carrot, parsley, bay leaves (sauteed)
1 pt./1600 ml. Weeping Radish Springbock
2-3 onions thinly sliced
1-1/2 lb./ 750g red potatoes, thinly sliced
Fresh chopped rosemary, and a little butter

Sauté lambchops in a little hot fat with the vegetables. Pour on the beer and lightly braise the chops for a few minutes. Strain off the liquor and put chops aside. Saute onions very lightly until just soft, then layer with the potatoes to nearly fill a medium roasting dish. Pour over the beer liquid to reach just below the top layer. Top with a little butter and sprinkle with rosemary. Bake in a 375 degree oven for 45 minutes until the beer is almost absorbed and the potatoes tender. Place chops on top of potatoes and return to oven for about 10-15minutes. Serves 4

# The Weeping Radish Brewhaus

5301A N. Croatan Hwy.
Kitty Hawk, North Carolina

Uli Bennewitz, Owner (252) 261-0488
Kenny Bland, Chef

*The latest installment in the Weeping Radish family boasts an Old World-Style restaurant and pub with traditional Bavarian lunch and dinner and local delicacies. From their great beer and sinful beer bread to one of the only rotisserie ovens on the beach, The Weeping Radish Brewhaus in Kitty Hawk will surely be an enjoyable experience for all.*

## Velvet Cream of Butternut Squash Soup

2 lbs. butternut squash (3-4 squash)
1 lb. carrot
2 medium yellow onion
2 ea. apple (golden delicious preferred) or 1 c. apple sauce
¼ lb. whole butter
1 ea. cinnamon stick
1 tsp. ground clove
1 tsp. white pepper
½ tsp. cayenne pepper
½ tsp. paprika
¼ c. honey
½ c. Corolla Gold beer
¼ c. spiced rum
½ c. heavy cream
¼ c. brown sugar
1 qt. vegetable sock
1 tsp. salt

Peel, seed and dice the butternut squash and the apple. Peel and dice the onion and carrot. Put the squash and the carrot in a large heavy pot with the vegetable broth, cinnamon stick and salt. Simmer until tender, about 40 minutes. Discard the cinnamon stick.

In a sauté pan, melt the butter and gently cook the onion, stirring occasionally until they become soft, about 5 minutes. Add the apple and cook for another 5 minutes. Add the rum and reduce. Add the beer and simmer for 10 minutes, uncovered.

Remove the squash and carrot, then add it to the apple mixture. Reserve the vegetable broth in another container. Purée the vegetables in batches in a blender and return to the large heavy pot.

Over medium heat, add the spices and honey, stir. Add the brown sugar and cream, stir. Finally, add the reserved vegetable stock until a desired thickness is achieved. Simmer for 5 minutes, but do not boil. Add more salt if needed. Garnish with ground clove, chive or cilantro. Yields 2½ qts.

# Windmill Point Restaurant

## SS United States Lounge

Hwy. 158 Bypass, MP 16½
Nags Head, North Carolina

Dr. Sarah Forbes, M.D., Owner (252) 441-1535
Scott Ramm, Executive Chef

*From the spectacular sound view that bosts glorious sunsets on a nightly basis to the award-winning cuisine that Windmill Point is so famous for, Dr. Forbes has taken great pride in bringing the world's largest collection of memorabilia from the SS United States to carry on a standard of tradition.*

*Nautical themes are found throughout this elegantly appointed restaurant --from the navy linen napkins folded upright on the tables to the wooden captain's wheel and lit lanterns. The United States Lounge on the upper deck has a kidney-shaped bar with the original stools that once were on board the SS United States.*

*Dinners are served in the grand tradition of the luxury ocean liner with excellent service you would expect from such a fine restaurant. Their expanded award-winning menu features fresh local seafood, Iowa beef, veal, pasta, duck, home baked breads and exquisite desserts. A children's menu is also available. Banquets and catering available. Open year round for dinner.*

### Oysters Rockefeller

6 ea. oysters
2 oz. bacon, diced
1 oz. onion, diced
½ tsp. garlic, minced
4 oz. spinach
½ oz. Pernod
Salt to taste
Pepper to taste
1 oz. heavy cream
½ oz. Parmesan

Shuck oysters and leave on the ½ shell, render bacon, add onion and saute. Add garlic and spinach--deglaze with Pernod. Add heavy cream and Parmesan. Season with salt and pepper--mix together all ingredients well. Cook mixture--top oysters and bake till oyster is cooked.

*This recipe was given to me by Chef Stephen Duffey. I wanted to include it along with some of the other great recipes that are in this book. I know you will enjoy this one.*

## *Pecan & Pepper Crusted Salmon*
## *W/ Satiny Chardonnay & Cream Cheese Sauce*

4 6oz. skinless salmon filets
¾ cup chopped pecan
1 T. cracked black pepper
**Combine:**
8 oz. cream cheese
4 oz. heavy cream
2 oz. Chardonnay wine
1/8 tsp. salt
white pepper to taste

Combine last 5 ingredients in medium sauce pan over medium low heat stirring frequently. When hot, thicken with cornstarch slurry if needed. In ten inch sauté pan, add ¾ cup vegetable oil and place over medium heat. Mix pecans & pepper and press onto both sides of salmon and place into pan. Cook until golden brown on both sides. Place ladle of sauce on plate and lay salmon on top.
Chicken, tuna or veal will work well also.

*I am including this recipe that was given to me by Chefs Franko Montesi and Zia S. Montesi. His restaurant is no longer located on the Outer Banks but I thought you would still enjoy his Rosemary Chicken recipe.*

## *Franko's Rosemary Chicken*

*Sautéed Boneless Chicken Breast with Roasted Garlic, Fresh Rosemary, Plum Tomatoes, Scallions and a Fresh Basil Leaf and Finished in a White Wine Sauce.*

Dredge boneless chicken breast in seasoned flour
1 tablespoon chopped roasted garlic
2 plum tomatoes halved and sliced
¼ cup chopped scallions
2-4 whole basil leaves
¼ cup white wine
2 tablespoons olive oil

Dredge chicken in seasoned flour and brown in hot olive oil and rosemary, turn chicken over and add all ingredients. Cook till done. Finish with white wine.

To order additional copies of **Outer Banks Cuisine, A Sampling Of Our Restaurants with Recipes**, complete the information below

Ship to: (please print)
Name________________________________________
Address______________________________________
City, State, Zip_________________________________
Day Phone____________________________________

____copies of Outer Banks Cuisine, A Sampling
Of Our Restaurants with Recipes @ $ 8.95 each $______

Postage and handling @ $ 2.00 per book $______

Enclosed is my check or money order for $______

Make checks payable to and send to:
Dirt Enterprises
P.O. Box 262
Harbinger, North Carolina 27941
(252) 491-2403

---

To order additional copies of **Outer Banks Cuisine, A Sampling Of Our Restaurants with Recipes**, complete the information below

Ship to: (please print)
Name________________________________________
Address______________________________________
City, State, Zip_________________________________
Day Phone____________________________________

____copies of Outer Banks Cuisine, A Sampling
Of Our Restaurants with Recipes @ $ 8.95 each $______

Postage and handling @ $ 2.00 per book $______

Enclosed is my check or money order for $______

Make checks payable to and send to:
Dirt Enterprises
P.O. Box 262
Harbinger, North Carolina 27941
(252) 491-2403

---